Reset

Your Mindset

Reset

Your Mindset

David L. Washco

For information, on reprints, permissions, etc., please contact author at dlwashco@gmail.net.

Published by Harbor of Wisdom, 6917 Pin Oaks Dr., Denver NC 28037 USA First Edition

ISBN: 979-8-218-71243-3

Published by Harbor of Wisdom

DEDICATION

To my beloved bride, Amy Washco. From the moment we
first met, it was evident that you were a divine blessing in my
life. Your presence has been a profound testament to the
grace of God, illuminating the path of unconditional love.
With deep gratitude, I acknowledge your invaluable
contributions to this book, our enduring marriage, and the
cherished bonds of our family. Your unwavering support and
belief in me have been constant pillars. I am endlessly
thankful for your love and companionship.

ACKNOWLEDGMENTS

In writing a book about renewing your mindset, I first want to honor the people who helped shape mine. These mentors, friends, and anchors have poured into my life, consistently challenging me, encouraging me, and walking alongside me as I've grown into a better husband, father, and leader in my community. Their influence has left fingerprints on every page of this journey:

Stephen Washco, Charlie Van Hecke, Rick Hamby, Charlie Swanson, Tom Rolen, Chris Cerrito, Susie Huggins, Bob Thompson, Frank Drendel, Sandi Walters, Joseph Condeelis, Bruce Schronce, Hanshi Danny McCall, Joseph McClellan, Wayne DeLoriea, Savannah Washco, and Riley Washco.

"Tell me and I forget, teach me and I may remember, involve me and I learn." – Benjamin Franklin

CONTENTS

INTRODUCTION

Let's cut through the crap and get right to it. Life principles are simple; they are just not easy to live out. From the moment I drew my first breath, I embarked on an underdog's journey. I was born four weeks premature, which, back in the 1960s, almost guaranteed a rough start in life. Survival rates for premature infants were far lower then, and my fragile lungs marked the beginning of a lifelong battle with asthma. But that was just the beginning.

Adoption, even under the best of circumstances, presents its own set of challenges. I arrived in this world blissfully unaware of my circumstances. My adoptive parents were caught off guard. They had expected several more weeks to prepare for the arrival of a healthy, full-term baby boy. There was no crib, no diapers, and the nursery was far from put together. Beyond the physical preparation, my adoptive parents had little time to wrap their minds around the fact that the healthy baby boy they were expecting was, in reality a preemie with potential risks and challenges. Yet, they rose to the occasion with unwavering determination and embraced me wholeheartedly. Perhaps my early entrance into the world planted the seed of my lifelong obsession with punctuality. I always strive to arrive 15 minutes ahead of schedule wherever I go.

Early on, my dad recognized my tenacity and thirst for achievement. Having a desire to quench my thirst, he was driven to equip me for life, imbuing every activity we undertook with valuable lessons. We couldn't just *play* with the Tinker Toys, we aimed to see how *high* we could build them before they toppled. There was no looking up at the sky at the clouds and identifying silly shapes; we delved into discussions on the difference between stratus, cirrus, and cumulonimbus formations. My first driving lesson involved a massive transport van on a gravel road, simulating snowy road conditions, teaching me to steer into a skid to regain control.

As a boy, I didn't understand or appreciate the value of what he was doing or the important life skills he was teaching me. Now, as a man with children of my own, I long for his presence and would give anything to receive his instructions. I lost my dad early in life but I feel his impact remains with me daily.

Maybe it was divine foreshadowing that drove dad to impart his wisdom and knowledge during my formative years. Early on, he intentionally provided me with a road map for life. I lost my dad, but I was determined not to lose his voice and guidance. In my early twenties I began journaling, capturing invaluable lessons from him. Documenting motivational quotes from mentors and the profound messages from countless books. This brought me comfort and a sense of stability. As a father, husband, and mentor, it became my personal mission to preserve dad's life-changing knowledge and wisdom. To this day, I continue to journal the lessons learned from both successes and failures.

I have always been fascinated by individuals who achieve their dreams and goals faster and more significantly than others. I'm intrigued by those who rise above adversity, contrasting sharply with those who seem trapped in a cycle of misery. What distinguishes someone who radiates joy in every circumstance from another who seems to drain the energy from a room?

So, what's the point of all this? I always knew that one day I would have a family of my own. Unfortunately, they would never know my dad or the invaluable lessons he imparted to me. Like my dad, I've been driven to share the wisdom I've gathered to ensure his legacy lives on through me, benefiting my family and others. I heard my dad say a thousand times, "Do unto others as you would have them do unto you." If his love and teachings show up in my footprints and are documented in this book to help family and others, his legacy will endure.

By now, you are probably wondering why I chose the title "Reset"? I spent most of my career in various sales roles in corporate America. Like any true salesman, I will start by asking a couple of qualifying questions to illustrate why this title is fitting and, more importantly, why you should continue reading.

Life's principles are simple; they just are not easy. Wouldn't it be remarkable if you were "aware" of the red flags that lead to mistakes and heartache sooner rather than later? Imagine being able to discern the warning signs or distractions that many people inevitably encounter. Wouldn't it be beneficial to know which people in your life to avoid and the ones in which to invest? Consider the simplicity of distinguishing truth from trend and the ability to navigate life's potholes more efficiently without colliding and causing harm to others.

The lessons I have learned from my dad and mentors have profound and practical applications. This book isn't solely about knowing what to do when you reach a crossroads. Sometimes, you must ask if you're in the right vehicle, on the correct road, and in the right state of mind. Making mistakes and learning from them is essential for progress and success. Learning from the mistakes of others is far less painful. In essence, this book will set you on the right path to living a rewarding and meaningful life. Your current station in life, your past, your level of education, and even the setbacks you've encountered do not have to be a hindrance. Your perspective, mindset, and journey toward behavioral change begin with your choices today. Remember, YOUR

3

life is not a dress rehearsal. I challenge you to "reset" your mindset and recalibrate your internal compass to achieve your personal best in the only life you've been given.

So, will today be your "Day One" to a more significant life, or just another "One day…"

CHAPTER 1
TACTICS OR PRINCIPLES

Tactics: short-term methods or maneuvers used to achieve immediate results. They are situational, often reactive, and driven by external goals or pressures.

Principles: Fundamental truths and internal convictions that guide consistent behavior, regardless of the situation. They stem from who you are, not what you want in the moment.

The day after returning from the President's Club award trip and experiencing the honor of being recognized as *Pharmaceutical Representative of the Year* at Searle Pharmaceuticals, something happened that stopped me in my tracks. A companywide voicemail detailing my previous year's achievements went out. Shortly afterward, I received a phone call from a crafty sales colleague of mine with whom I butted heads many times over the years regarding our different approach to sales. He called to ask me, "David, do you have 10 minutes to share your strategy on how you earned Representative of the Year?" My immediate thought was, "Really? You believe I can condense my journey from last place among 1,400 representatives to the nation's pinnacle rank in a mere ten minutes?" That's when I realized this guy was fixated on "TACTICS" rather than

"PRINCIPLES." His request further confirmed my suspicions of his "it's all about me" mentality.

This encounter was profoundly enlightening. It prompted me to step back and delve deep into understanding why his seemingly simple request was so problematic. There is a distinct time and place for both tactics and principles. *Principles* are the involuntary expressions of our values, etched into our way of life. *Tactics*, on the other hand, are the tools we employ to conquer and attain specific goals in the short run. When working with others, if tactics are the driving force, people unconsciously perceive a "lack of authenticity or hidden agenda in your actions, often triggering subliminal associations of insincerity. Rarely do tactics align with the concept of a win-win scenario. The cost to rebuild trust is substantial in terms of time, effort, and resources once it has been eroded due to perceived tactics. Principles, conversely, are intrinsically linked with lifestyle, authenticity, trustworthiness, and a greater good for all. Principled individuals are respected, even if others do not share the same principles, because they recognize such convictions as genuine.

Far too often, we are enticed by the allure of the short game: How quickly can we achieve our immediate goals? This fixation is frequently driven by external pressures or our desires for instant gratification. We've all encountered moments when our bosses pressured us to meet their demands. To relieve the immediate pressure and comply with their requests swiftly, we employed tactical maneuvers to meet their expectations. These short-term actions provide momentary relief but can disrupt the momentum needed to achieve our long-term goals. We often fail to recognize that what we do today has a profound influence on our long-term success. Our present actions shape our future.

The truth is that it's about lifestyle! I'm not talking about clothes, cars, homes, or possessions. I am talking about applying and *living* your life principles in all areas of your life every day. Just as air is essential for the lungs and blood for the heart, principles are vital for achieving your personal best. Earning Pharmaceutical Representative of the Year was a direct outcome of living by my principles and publicly declaring my intentions of committing to "do no harm and always recommend what is best for the patient." At the age of twenty-six, I was a novice in the cardiovascular sales industry, surrounded by colleagues who were predominately in their forties and fifties, with an average tenure of eleven years. I needed to quickly differentiate myself and gain the trust of physicians to succeed in my territory. My strategy was straightforward: make it known that I dedicated a minimum of thirty minutes each morning studying outcome trials, not just of my products, but my competitors' as well. I vowed to remain impartial and always prioritize the patient's well-being over any specific product, even if it meant endorsing a competitor's brand.

This approach became my marketing positioning or brand. While some physicians quickly recognized and appreciated my offering, others were more hesitant and tested my credibility multiple times. Nevertheless, within my first year, I earned the trust of most physicians, becoming a reliable resource and trusted advisor for effective methods in reducing morbidity and mortality in cardiovascular patients. Midway through the year, my territory, once languishing at the bottom in rankings, surged to the mid seven-hundreds out of fourteen hundred representatives. During a sales meeting in July, my manager presented our territory rankings on a flip chart. To hold myself accountable, when the meeting was over, I asked for the rankings page and I taped it inside my car's trunk lid, making it highly visible each time I retrieved samples. It was a constant reminder and a potent motivator, even if it earned curious glances in the medical office parking lots.

Achieving desired results requires unwavering commitment, and there are no shortcuts. Illusionary shortcuts only delay and undermine your endeavors and resources. While "The Hare and the Tortoise" may be an Aesop fable for children, its message of slow and steady progress is a fundamental truth that should be embraced early to dispel life's myths about seeking shortcuts.

You may be wondering if I shared my strategy with my colleague. I am an open book, willing to assist anyone who seeks to grow. Whether they choose to accept advice or not is their prerogative. My crafty sales colleague had a short-lived career in pharmaceutical sales, which came to a swift end when he approached a physician, requesting the physician write a prescription for his brand of medicine because he was "just one script away from winning a performance trip."

The outcome of *principles* is a win-win perspective, while *tactics,* by nature, have a win-lose conclusion.

CHAPTER 2
PROTECTIVE OR PERSPECTIVE

Protective: Protective is the instinct to shield your beliefs, experiences, or identity from challenge or scrutiny—often driven by fear of being wrong, misunderstood, or vulnerable. It manifests as defensiveness, closed-mindedness, or dismissiveness when faced with opposing viewpoints.

Perspective: Perspective is the ability to see beyond your own viewpoint and appreciate the context, background, and meaning behind others' experiences. It involves curiosity, humility, and the willingness to understand before being understood.

Why does the arduous task of attentively listening to another person's insights, convictions, and viewpoints remain so challenging for us? Particularly when they diverge from our own. I comprehend that many of you are currently assuring yourselves that you excel in the art of listening to others. Can you honestly claim to be absent of the subtle eyeroll when confronted with a differing viewpoint? Could it be that you merely wear the façade of a listener, concealing your true intent to expound your "correct" perspective at the next moment of the speaker's inhaling breath? The pressing query we must pose to ourselves is this: "Why do we zealously guard our beliefs to the extent that we are unwilling to lend a genuine ear to others' perspectives?

It is my experience that people typically shun the embrace of alternative viewpoints for one of three primary motives:

1. Being averse to the possibility of encountering opinions that might challenge your experiences or beliefs.
2. Making an erroneous assumption that they possess the knowledge to defend a position when, in reality, they lack the shrewdness to defend their stance and dread the possibility of being proven incorrect.
3. They have achieved the status of an expert in their field and disdain, squandering their precious time on those who exhibit a lack of open-mindedness.

Confidence in one's beliefs, or being well-versed in them, should ideally bestow upon us the capacity to be open-minded and possess the ability to listen genuinely, especially when the other party demonstrates a readiness to broaden their perspective.

How do we pursue an effective means to convey the paramount importance of open-mindedness and an eagerness to embrace diverse perspectives? While working out at the gym, a vivid vision began to crystallize in my mind. Let me offer an analogy that has the potential to make a profound impact when explaining the value of being receptive to other people's viewpoints.

This doesn't simply mean letting the other person speak first. When you approach a conversation with a sincere intent to understand their perspective, you tear down the walls, barriers, and defenses they might have erected. Can you entertain the possibility that two individuals can contemplate the same event or object, embracing differing perspectives, and BOTH be accurate? Remarkably, that transpires more frequently than one might conclude.

Consider the allegory of the brass bell. Within our nation, two revered groups of individuals would respond differently to the query, "Would you be willing to ring this bell?" One faction would emphatically proclaim, "Indeed," while the other would recoil from the notion! Permit me to pose the following queries:

1. Are we in mutual agreement that this is unequivocally a bell? To this, both groups would vigorously agree, "Yes."
2. Would we unanimously consent that this bell is crafted from some variant of metal? Once more, both factions would concur.
3. Do we all ascribe to the belief that this bell possesses the capacity to emit a resounding noise when rung? Again, both groups would emphatically respond, "Yes."
4. Do we concur that this bell could be situated on a farm, in a church, or even aboard a vessel? Unanimously, both would affirm "Yes."

Illustration 1

The consensus on the bell's identity, attributes, and potential habitats is indisputable. Why, then, does one faction eagerly grasp the bell's cord while the other retreats in apprehension? The answer lies in perspective. In this narrative, one faction comprises trainees from the elite Navy SEALs. To a Navy SEAL trainee, ringing the bell symbolizes FAILURE! It signifies surrendering to the rigors of their training program. When a SEAL trainee approaches the precipice of their endurance, they summon the strength to drag themselves to the bell and sound it thrice, a solemn proclamation of their voluntary withdrawal from the program.

The other contingent comprises valiant cancer survivors. For them, ringing the bell signifies TRIUMPH! These survivors have triumphed over the travails of cancer treatment and stand as beacons of victory. For them, ringing the bell marks a celebratory milestone in their grueling journey. The same bell, yet perceived through divergent prisms. Picture these two groups, unbeknownst to one another, engaging in a discourse about the symbolism of the bell. They would never be harmonized in their understanding without the practice of "seeking first to understand, then to be understood." Neither group invalidates the other's perspective; they simply occupy different vantage points. As these two groups partake in mutual listening, it becomes increasingly likely that the Navy SEAL trainee might cultivate a more profound empathy for the cancer survivor. Conversely, the cancer survivor might better comprehend why the Navy SEAL trainee remains opposed to the bell.

Significantly, an extraordinary transformation unfolds. Neither group finds it necessary to amend their belief system or discredit their personal experiences. Yet, a newfound mutual respect blossoms, previously absent, all due to the practice of "seeking first to understand, then to be understood."

When you unshackle yourself from the fortress of your convictions and embrace the *perspectives* of others, you are liberated from being *protective* of your viewpoints.

CHAPTER 3
SUCCESS OR SIGNIFICANCE

Success: Success is the achievement of personal goals or milestones, often measured by external accolades, performance metrics, or social validation. It is typically self-focused, fleeting, and defined by the standards of the world.

Significance: Significance is the impact you make on others and the legacy you leave behind. It is rooted in purpose, fueled by service, and measured by lasting influence rather than temporary achievement.

It may be time to consider a paradigm shift if you've been relentlessly chasing success. Let's venture into territory many never explore: the space between **what looks good now** and **what lasts forever**.

In our culture, the word *success* echoes through our ears 10,000 times louder than the quieter—but far more powerful—concept of *significance*. It's plastered across social media, celebrated in headlines, and tied to everything from wealth to status to titles. But let me ask you this: have you been aiming too low without even realizing it?

Many people fixate on acquiring success, often with a warped definition. We're led to believe that success is the ultimate destination. But what if it's not? What if success is only a vehicle—a steppingstone—meant to carry you toward something far greater: "significance"?

Success ends with you. It can vanish when your career ends, when the applause fades, or when your title no longer holds weight. For some, it fades even earlier—when the next person breaks your record or when the company you built your reputation on no longer exists.

Significance, on the other hand, begins where success leaves off. It's what remains when the trophies are forgotten, and the job plaques collect dust in the attic. It's the stories people tell about how you impacted their lives, the lessons you passed down, and the light you brought into dark places.

Zig Ziglar, a man whose teachings deeply shaped me, once said: "You are endowed with the seeds of greatness. You are designed for accomplishment. You are engineered for success."

Those words helped me discover my identity in my early years. But with time, reflection, and spiritual maturity, I've come to update his final line to something I believe Zig himself would endorse: *"You are engineered for significance."*

From that realization, I developed a personal mantra that's guided me ever since: *"You are created on purpose, for a purpose. The purpose of life is to live a life of purpose. There is no pain or trial in life greater than your purpose."*

In today's world, we are constantly told to *be the best.* But if you look through the lens of Scripture, you won't find a command to pursue worldly greatness or top-ranking titles. The world screams, *you're only valuable if you win,* but the Word whispers something deeper: *you're valuable because of who created you—and why.*

We're conditioned to believe that we are insignificant unless we're valedictorians, record-setters, millionaires, or first-place finishers. "Nobody remembers second place," we're told. Really?

As a lifelong Philadelphia Eagles fan, I vividly remember their 1980 Super Bowl run. That team had the fewest points allowed in the NFL all season—only 222. Yet, they finished second in the league. I still remember that season, not because they were the best, but because it mattered to me.

And let's be honest—how many of our once-precious accolades are sitting in a forgotten box somewhere? I once became the first person in Dictaphone Corporation's 100-year history to hit $1 million in sales. It was a proud moment... until the next year, when someone broke my record. And today, that company doesn't even exist. If success is your goal, you're building your life on sand.

Here's the truth: striving to be *the best* isn't inherently wrong. Excellence honors the gifts God gave you. But when your pursuit of "best" is driven by insecurity, ego, or external validation, you're playing a game that never ends. There's always someone faster, richer, more intelligent, or newer.

Instead, aim to *be YOUR best*. That's a goal grounded in grace. It means using what God placed in your hands to its fullest potential—not to outshine others, but to honor your design. This mindset is reflected in countless biblical stories. God doesn't measure our worth by where we rank, but by how we use what we've been given. Remember the parable of the talents? The master didn't reward the servant who made *the most*—he rewarded the ones who did the *most with what they had*.

When my daughter gives her all to study for a math test and earns a C+, I'm not disappointed. I'm proud—because she was faithful with her effort. The result matters less than the heart behind it.

Success is an ever-moving target. It changes with the trends, the metrics, and the mood of the crowd. And it often breeds an insatiable hunger for more. Like the farmer in the parable who said, "I don't want all the land—just the land next to mine," the pursuit of success is never satisfied.

Significance, however, satisfies the soul.

When you live for significance, your question shifts from *"How can I be impressive?"* to *"How can I make a difference?"* You begin to ask:

- Whose life can I improve today?
- What value can I bring to this moment?
- How can I use my success as a platform to serve others?

Those who make this shift—from chasing applause to choosing purpose—don't just *do well.* The good they do benefits others. And in doing so, they leave a legacy that outlives them.

Success focuses on the self. Significance flows from a sincere concern for others. And when you build a life on significance, you won't need trophies or applause to validate your worth. Your life will speak for itself—through the people you've lifted, the lives you've shaped, and the purpose you've fulfilled. So don't chase *success.* Live a life of *significance.*

CHAPTER 4
CONTRIBUTE OR COMMIT

Contribute: To give or participate in a limited or partial way, often without long-term investment or full responsibility. Contribution plays a supporting role—it adds value, but with boundaries. It involves doing what is convenient or expected, without necessarily embracing the full weight of the outcome.

Commit: To be fully invested—emotionally, mentally, and often sacrificially—in a cause, relationship, or mission. Commitment involves taking ownership, staying present through adversity, and aligning your actions with long-term goals.

Whenever someone tries to convince me of their commitment, I'm reminded of a story I once heard...

> A chicken and a pig were walking up the driveway on a large farm, marveling at how fortunate they were to live in such a beautiful place. They began discussing ways they could express their gratitude to Farmer Jed for allowing them to live on his farm. It didn't take very long for the chicken to come up with an idea. She excitedly suggested to the pig, "We should make Farmer Jed breakfast! We can prepare him a wonderful ham and egg breakfast." The pig,

however, immediately responded, "No way. For you it's just a contribution. For me, it would be a commitment!"

That story has stuck with me for years—because it perfectly captures the difference between showing up and *signing on*. We've all found ourselves in situations—whether in a job, a relationship, or a group project—where we feel like we're the only one truly committed.

Most people can relate to this from high school. Picture it: awkward dances, questionable fashion choices, and of course, the drama of teenage romance. But perhaps nothing was more universally dreaded than hearing the teacher say, "Class, this is your group assignment." Every student groaned—not because they feared the work, but because they already knew how it would unfold. One person would inevitably carry the weight, while others would contribute just enough to get credit. It's the classic contrast: contribution versus commitment. And sadly, it doesn't end in high school.

The real challenge in adulthood is recognizing someone's level of commitment before it's tested—because by the time you realize they were only contributing, it's often too late.

We hear phrases like "You're only as strong as your weakest link" or, as my martial arts instructor says, "How you do anything is how you do everything." This speaks to more than just habits—it reflects your character. If you treat small tasks with care and dedication, you'll likely bring that same commitment to larger responsibilities. But, if you cut corners in the small things, that attitude usually carries over.

Wouldn't it be more productive and less painful if we could spot true commitment from the beginning?

Take marriage, for example. Poor communication is often cited as a significant factor toward divorce. Still, I believe that at the root of poor communication is a lack of clarity about each person's level of commitment. If you're unsure where the other person stands, it's challenging to communicate with honesty or confidence.

Amy and I both experienced divorce in our early twenties. Those were incredibly painful seasons, but Amy often refers to them as our "starter marriages"—not to minimize them, but to acknowledge the hard lessons we never want to repeat. After those experiences, both of us told God that if we were ever to marry again, it would be with someone fully committed from the start.

And we meant it. After just a few dates, Amy and I realized our relationship had potential. So, we had the "big conversation." This time, we were wiser. We knew that trying to change someone wasn't fair or realistic. As Benjamin Franklin famously said, "Keep your eyes wide open before marriage, and half shut afterward."

Amy made it clear: there would be no tolerance for alcohol abuse, drug use, or infidelity. I agreed—and added one more boundary: the word "divorce" would never be used. Not as a threat. Not in frustration. Not even as a joke.

That mutual clarity gave us the foundation we needed to build a marriage marked by trust, safety, and openness— not just for us, but also for our children.

That same principle applies in any meaningful partnership. Whether you're hiring someone, leading a team, or starting a new relationship, set expectations early. And ask the right questions:

- What are you willing to sacrifice for this goal?
- How will you stay engaged when things get hard?
- How does this commitment rank among your other priorities?
- What can others expect from you, and what do you expect in return?
- What does full commitment mean to you in this context?

These questions act as a litmus test. They're not just about collecting information—they set the tone. They help you determine whether someone is truly invested or simply checking the box. They also create a culture of clarity, alignment, and mutual understanding before the onset of pressure.

In the long run, these conversations can prevent conflict, minimize confusion, and help you build something that's not just functional, but flourishing.

Anyone can *contribute*. Few are willing to *commit*. But if you're building something that matters, you don't need more chickens. You need pigs.

CHAPTER 5
CERTAINTY OR CLARITY

Certainty: The emotional assurance that arises from perceived truth or tangible evidence—an anchor in times of chaos, often sought to create a sense of control and comfort.

Clarity: The ability to understand and communicate with precision and simplicity—a guiding compass through complexity.

As I pen these words, our world stands at the crossroads of a profound transformation. Three years have elapsed since the relentless onset of the COVID-19 pandemic, leaving an indelible mark on our daily existence. At its inception, this virus triggered a cascade of governmental measures: mandated shutdowns for "non-essential employees," travel restrictions spanning borders and states. Stay-at-home orders persisted, turning board games, bicycles, and outdoor gear into treasures. At the same time, swamped by a surge in home improvement projects, hardware stores raced to replenish their inventory. The RV industry also experienced an unprecedented boom as families sought solace in outdoor adventures amid the confinement. Amidst this chaos, a daily barrage of conflicting information on curbing the virus's spread. Guidance on using masks, social distancing, vaccine efficacy, and the necessity of booster shots further muddied the waters. We may have gleaned the virus's origins, albeit through the fog of media obfuscation, but the circumstances of its release remained shrouded in controversy.

Over the past two years, Americans have experienced a unique era in history that has exposed the fragility of our civil liberties, leaving many people feeling disillusioned. Who could have foreseen the United States government permitting the destruction of major cities and businesses during riots, instructing law enforcement to stand down and refrain from intervening? We've long tolerated our "first responders" enduring meager wages, but did we ever anticipate witnessing the active defunding of law enforcement, an institution fundamental to our safety?

Once regarded as steadfast anchors, many sources of certainty are now revealed as mere mirages. Several beliefs and practices to which we clung before the pandemic have crumbled.

So, let me pose crucial questions: Have we dedicated too much of our energy to pursuing *certainty* while neglecting the pursuit of *clarity*? Or should we delve even deeper and question whether the certainty we once held was often built upon a shaky foundation of false clarity? Is our yearning for certainty rooted in a desire for an emotional sanctuary? In 1989, Henry J.M. Nouwen offered poignant insight:

> "The secular world around us is shouting, "We can take care of ourselves. We do not need God, the church, or a priest. We are in control. And if we are not, we must work harder to get in control. The problem is not a lack of faith but a lack of competence. If you are sick, you need a competent doctor; if you are poor, you need competent politicians; if there are technical problems, you need competent engineers; if there are wars, you need competent negotiators. God, the church, and the minister have been used for centuries to fill the gaps

of incompetence, but today, the gaps are being filled in other ways, and we no longer need spiritual answers to practical questions." Efficiency and control are the great aspirations of our society. Yet, loneliness, isolation, absence of friendship and intimacy, fractured relationships, boredom, feelings of emptiness and depression, and a profound sense of uselessness afflict millions of individuals in our success-oriented world."

When people seek direction, strive for advancement, crumble under adversity, and grapple with brokenness, they yearn for certainty, specifically, a sense of control. They desire answers that are clear, concise, and immediate. Yet, in their fervent quest for certainty, they are often trapped by the deceptive allure of false clarity.

Certainty, at its core, represents the allure of an assured fact. It is the reassuring pat on the back, the confident stride based on tangible evidence. It's an emotional state, an intoxicating cocktail of confidence, security, and control. When misunderstood, certainty can become a seductive mirage, an illusion of control in an uncertain world. It's human nature to seek security and assurance, and in our quest for these comforts, we sometimes grasp onto false certainty. This misappropriation can show up in many forms:

Overconfidence: When we mistake confidence for certainty, we become closed to new ideas and perspectives. We may disregard valuable input from others and stunt our personal growth by believing we have all the answers.

Rigidity: Clinging to unwavering beliefs and refusing to entertain doubt or ambiguity can impede personal growth. It restricts our ability to adapt and learn from life's experiences.

Avoidance Risk: Fear of the unknown often leads us to seek unwavering certainty, preventing us from taking calculated risks that can foster personal development. *People will take more risks to avoid a loss than to realize a gain.* Growth often requires stepping out of our comfort zones.

In stark contrast, clarity emerges as the quality of being easily understood – a guiding light piercing the fog of confusion. It is the art of precise expression, ensuring that ideas are remembered, grasped, and accurately conveyed.

While certainty craves the weight of evidence, clarity seeks the simplicity of understanding. It doesn't drown us in the minutiae of facts and figures but offers a clear path through the network of complexity.

Consider, for a moment, a different narrative – one of a dedicated teacher sharing her story with me one day after church service. This teacher, let's call her Sarah, works with a group of underprivileged children in a run-down school. She understands that the path to empowerment for these children lies not in overwhelming them with certainty but in providing clarity in their education. Sara doesn't bombard her students with information; instead, she crafts easily understood lessons. She breaks down complex concepts into bite-sized pieces, patiently guiding her students through the maze of knowledge. She equips them with the clarity they need to navigate a world that often seems stacked against them. Sara appears to be fighting upstream in a system that wants to teach our children "how they should feel" instead of "how to problem solve."

The central concept conveyed here pertains to the symbiotic relationship between certainty and clarity in the context of life's journey. Visualize them as two valuable tools at our disposal. Certainty can be likened to an anchor, stabilizing us when confronted with adversity and imparting a sense of self-assurance in our actions. However, we must exercise caution in our pursuit of certainty, recognizing that it may not always be attainable. In such instances, it is prudent to rely on a well-defined plan and forge ahead.

On the other hand, clarity operates as a compass, invaluable when navigating through periods of ambiguity and perplexity. It possesses the ability to simplify intricate situations, ensuring our graceful and purposeful navigation through the tumultuous waters of life. Hence it is advantageous to maintain a degree of *certainty* to provide stability, yet we must avoid becoming entangled in an endless quest for it. Instead, let *clarity* be what we strive for to serve as our guide throughout life's journey.

CHAPTER 6
DESIRE OR HUNGER

Desire: A longing or wish to attain something—a spark that ignites interest or ambition. Desire is often sincere but passive, subject to convenience and comfort, and lacking the urgency or sacrifice needed to sustain action when difficulty arises.

Hunger: An unrelenting, internal drive fueled by urgency, necessity, or conviction—an insatiable craving that refuses to be ignored. Hunger compels action, endures setbacks, and perseveres beyond comfort, excuses, or obstacles. It is not merely wanting but doing.

As a high school teenager just diagnosed with dyslexia, I found myself seated at the conference table with my parents and the purported expert of the learning facility. I still vividly recall the moment when those unforgettable, indelible words pierced the room: "He should be prepared for a life of struggle, hardship, and mediocrity."

As a preemie child who had tenaciously clung to life, you can picture that these words did not merely irk me; they ignited an internal fire that still burns to this day.

But what truly set my spirit ablaze were the cautionary words of warning directed at my parents that resounded: "There is a good chance he will never see the light of high school graduation. The prospect of college is even more elusive. Please prepare him but understand that if he manages to set foot on a college campus by some miraculous twist of fate, don't expect him to survive the first semester."

I remembered these words during my Christmas break as I concluded my freshman Fall semester of college. As I sat on the brick hearth fireplace in our house, conversing with my mom about my final exam experiences, tears welled up in her eyes, prompting me to stop sharing and ask what was wrong. Amidst her tears, she confided, "I didn't think you would make it through your first semester."

To this day, I grapple with whether her disbelief or the haunting echoes of the expert's grim prophecy triggered a seismic shift within me. This seismic shift catapulted me from mere desire to a ravenous hunger, propelling me into a realm of unwavering discipline and an unparalleled drive to attain my loftiest goals.

In the intricate maze of human emotions and aspirations, two words often intertwine, used interchangeably to describe one's level of enthusiasm for achievement: "desire" and "hunger." At first glance, these two concepts may seem synonymous, but in reality, they have distinct meanings that silently shape our outcomes or lack thereof. People often use the term "desire" when they want others to believe in their commitment, yet their dedication is as steadfast as a kamikaze pilot on his tenth mission. Desire represents our present stance or feeling toward an outcome, but it lacks the power to guarantee progress. Desire alone might leave us rooted in place, yearning for change but unwilling to take the necessary steps to bring it to fruition.

On the other hand, the individual who embodies "hunger" exudes an unmistakable craving or urgency that defies explanation and appears virtually unstoppable. Hunger is an active force, a relentless drive that propels one into action, compelling the pursuit of goals with unwavering determination. Unlike desire, hunger is not just a fleeting sentiment; it's the tangible evidence of action, the fuel that powers us toward our goals.

Picture desire as the flickering flame of a candle, capable of illuminating a room but easily extinguishable by the slightest breeze. The initial spark ignites our ambitions, but it often needs more endurance to withstand adversity or the tests of time. Desire may make us wish for change, but it doesn't necessarily supply the fortitude to weather the storms of life and carry us across the finish line.

In stark contrast, hunger is the relentless blaze of a roaring furnace. It burns bright and hot, impervious to the winds of doubt and setbacks. Hunger is the force that propels us to take action, even when the path is treacherous, and the odds are stacked against us. It's an inner fire that refuses to be extinguished, an unquenchable thirst for progress that drives us to push beyond our limits.

Living and embracing the life of a dedicated martial artist, the perpetual inner battle between mere desire and unwavering hunger becomes glaringly honest each time I face the challenge of my next level of testing. On my journey toward attaining my third-degree black belt, the rank of Sandan, I was presented with the unique challenge: a fire walk. For those unfamiliar with firewalking, it is an ancient ritual with a rich history spanning centuries. Diverse cultures worldwide have adopted this practice, which is rooted in various traditions. All these firewalking rituals epitomize courage, faith, and strength. Firewalking symbolizes the profound capacity to confront one's deepest fears head-on and courageously embrace life's challenges. It transcends into a profound metaphor for mastering life's obstacles, including our inner insecurities and fears, through the sheer force of will or, more aptly put, "hunger." It serves as a powerful symbol of unlocking the boundless potential within us and embracing the limitless realm of what is achievable.

The firewalk serves as a compelling illustration of the stark disparity between desire and hunger. Having participated in more than one firewalk, I've observed numerous individuals approach the scorching edge of 1200 to

1500-degree Fahrenheit coals, only to stand there and quietly turn around.

Distinguishing between desire and hunger isn't confined solely to life's monumental challenges; it also reveals itself in the smaller, everyday moments. Not too long ago, I began guiding a group of congregants through the profound twelve-week-long workbook study, "Experiencing God" by the venerable Henry Blackaby. This transformative study entails daily readings and reflective questions designed to foster a deeper connection with God. However, on week three, a seemingly simple task exposed the stark contrast between mere desire and actual hunger. The assignment for that day was deceptively straightforward: to sit with God for a mere thirty minutes and listen. When our class convened to discuss our week's activities, I began by openly confessing my struggle with this seemingly uncomplicated task. I recounted my repeated attempts to fulfill the assignment, only to be thwarted each time by unforeseen interruptions and distractions. I meticulously detailed my endeavors and why I was unable to complete those thirty precious minutes of communion with God.

In response, the class exhibited remarkable understanding, offering consolation and empathy, as many had also fallen short of completing the task. However, a palpable shift occurred in the room as I humbly admitted my shortcomings – that my actions revealed a heart that merely desired to be with God but lacked the unquenchable hunger to truly spend quality time in His presence. It was an admission that cut through the air like a blade, leading us to profound introspection.

If I had been truly hungry to spend time with God, I would have risen at 4 a.m., when the house lay in peaceful stillness, guaranteeing me more than thirty minutes of uninterrupted communion with God. My struggle was not a matter of external circumstances but a testament to the depth of my hunger or lack thereof.

This seemingly simple exercise was a powerful reminder that desire is fleeting and often bound by convenience and circumstance. In contrast, hunger is an unrelenting force, undeterred by obstacles and distractions, propelling us forward with an insatiable drive to connect, learn, and grow. In these humbling moments of self-awareness, we discover the true measure of our hunger, not just for spiritual growth but for any pursuit that truly matters.

CHAPTER 7
DEFEATED OR DEPLETED

Defeated: A mindset where surrender has already occurred. Defeat is not just physical exhaustion—it's the moment you choose to stop believing, to stop fighting, and accept that further effort is futile. It signals a giving up of the will to press on, often before your actual limits are reached.

Depleted: A state of temporary exhaustion—physically, mentally, or emotionally drained—but not empty. Depletion means you're running low, not running out. There is still something left in the tank, even if it takes everything in you to find it.

It was January 11th, 2020, a brisk forty-six-degree Saturday morning in North Carolina. While most people were sipping their hot coffee and watching their favorite TV shows in the warmth of their homes, I was on day two of my three-day Nidan blackbelt test. I just finished a grueling three-mile timed run, followed by thirty minutes of push-ups, sit-ups, squats, a fireman's carry through wooded trails, and a series of required memorization drills (having to be stated with perfection) all while being hosed down with cold water. I was now about to face the next phase of my testing: grappling opponents in the elements of the outdoors.

As the group of senior black belts watched, my first opponent came at me with nothing to lose. Fortunately for me, I'd grappled with him many times before and knew he had a vulnerability to chokeholds. I forced him to tap out in under two minutes, but my victory came at a cost. My strategy of overpowering him to intimidate the next challenger left me exhausted. I sacrificed patience and technique, which left me fatigued, and my next opponent was eagerly awaiting his turn. He was much younger than I and a local high school wrestling athlete. I knew I needed to calm down and use technique over strength. After my allotted one-minute rest, we got it on. It was a battle of constant "move-counter-move," and as the minutes dragged on, my body began to betray me. Every muscle screamed with fatigue; every breath felt heavier than the last. My arms and legs struggled to obey the simplest of commands. By this point, I could barely see. Either mud or wet grass blurred my vision, so I relied solely on touch. That's when my brain did something dangerous: it began to rationalize.

"It's ok if you tap out," it whispered. You've been at this for two days straight. He just entered the ring. He's younger than you, and no one will fault you for giving up. No one really expected you to last this long. You showed great effort; surely, they will still let you keep testing for your next rank."

But I had been there many times before. I knew when the brain begins to rationalize, it's trying to do what it was designed for, survival. Not to win, but to survive. If that means shutting down to come back another day, then that's what it directs you to do. But this wasn't just any day; I was testing for my black belt, and there may not be another day.

In that moment, I had to make a critical decision: am I *depleted* or *defeated*? If I'm merely depleted, then I knew that there is always more in the tank. But if I am defeated, the brain has already won, and the battle is lost.

I wasn't about to give in. Digging deep, I reached into the reserves that only a fighter knows exist – those hidden places beyond physical endurance. My heart and soul demanded that my body keep going. "Finish strong!" I yelled, not just for myself but for everyone around me, so they'd know I wasn't done yet. The roar of the black belts encouraged me to press on. I reminded myself why I was here, why I'd sacrificed and trained for so long. Victory wasn't about beating my opponent – it was about conquering my limitations.

Finally, my opponent made a mistake, which allowed me to capitalize on locking him into an armbar from which there was no escape. With the slightest raise of my hip to add pressure, he tapped out.

I wanted to celebrate, but I had only sixty seconds to recover before my next opponent would zealously pursue my fatigued body.

The third match finished almost as quickly as it started. Much to my surprise, the choke-out took less than forty-five seconds. It took another forty-five seconds for me to become coherent and shake my opponent's hand out of respect.

With his fifty-plus years of teaching experience, my instructor intended me to keep fighting opponents until I was defeated. This served a two-fold purpose. First, it demonstrated to the blackbelt judges that I was living by Master Gichin Funakoshi's twenty rules of karate, particularly the first rule: "Karate begins and ends with respect." Even in the midst of a challenging trial and my one defeat, I was able to maintain a calm spirit. Second, the defeat wasn't the result of a choice to give up; it was a discovery of where my current limitations lie. And it was now for me to choose whether to push beyond my newly discovered limitations.

Most people theoretically know the difference between being defeated and depleted. Distinguishing the difference in the heat of the moment can have lifelong implications, depending on your response.

When you are *depleted*, your body, mind, or spirit may feel drained, but there is still fuel in the tank, even if it feels empty. You can push through depletion with grit, determination, and focus. It's temporary exhaustion, which can be overcome by tapping into reserves you didn't even know existed. Athletes, students, and leaders all experience depletion, where everything within them screams to stop, yet they press on and find that they have more to give.

On the other hand, *defeat* is final. It's not just about physical exhaustion; it's about the mind and spirit surrendering. Defeat occurs when we choose to give up, when we believe we've reached our limit and decide not to press forward. The body may still have strength left, but the decision to stop is mental. When defeat is self-chosen, it can be the end of growth and progress. Worse still, if we choose defeat without understanding whether we are truly at our limit, we rob ourselves of the chance to push through, grow stronger, and discover our capabilities.

Failing to recognize the difference between defeat and depletion can have profound consequences. Imagine someone on the verge of achieving a significant breakthrough, whether in business, athletics, or a personal challenge. Their body is exhausted, their mind is cloudy, and they start to feel the tug of rationalization—the subtle whispers telling them, "It's okay to stop now, you've done enough." If they mistake their depletion for defeat, they might quit too soon, never realizing how close they were to victory. I can't help but think of the "Never Give Up" cartoon, also known as the Digging for Diamonds, referring to a motivational image of two men in a diamond mine. The one on top is eagerly digging towards the diamonds while the one on the bottom is dejected and walking away, unaware he is only inches from discovering the diamonds.

Pushing through depletion leads to new levels of strength and endurance, both mentally and physically. It builds resilience, shapes character and fosters the confidence that comes from knowing you can persevere through even the most difficult of trials. On the other hand, surrendering to defeat can create a pattern of giving up when things get tough, reinforcing a mindset of limitation rather than possibility.

How can we learn to recognize whether we're depleted or truly defeated? There are at least four critical indicators. The first is physical signs. Depletion often manifests as fatigue, but you may still find bursts of energy if you dig deep. If you notice that you can still move, even if it's slow and painful, you're likely just depleted. Defeat, however, feels like your body has shut down entirely. There is no capacity to continue, even with effort. A second indicator would be your mental dialogue. Pay attention to your thoughts. Depletion often involves thoughts of struggle but also of perseverance. You may think, "This is hard, but I can do it." Defeat, on the other hand, is when the mind starts justifying quitting. If your thoughts shift to "I can't go on" or "It's okay to stop now," that's a sign that you may be choosing defeat. A third signal would be your emotional state. When you're depleted, you may feel frustrated or overwhelmed, but there's still a desire to keep moving. Defeat feels like resignation, a sense of finality. The desire to push through fades, replaced by acceptance of failure. A fourth indicator is your external circumstances. Consider the environment you're in and whether external pressures are influencing your decision to give up. Sometimes, the body's exhaustion is influenced by factors such as lack of sleep, stress, or hunger—conditions that can be alleviated.

A meaningful life lesson: Do not listen to society's norms when it comes to the pressure of defeat. Defeat does not automatically translate as "failure." My instructor is famous for saying, "Win or learn!" If you learn from defeat, there is redeeming value. If you do not learn from it, then you have indeed failed.

Defeat isn't always negative. Sometimes a defeat helps you understand where your actual limitations lie. However, it's crucial to ensure that defeat is not a result of giving up prematurely. Every defeat should serve as a learning moment—an opportunity to reflect, assess, and return stronger.

When I reached that moment of choice in my black belt test, I realized I was not defeated; I was simply exhausted. I had more in me, and I could still give more. And when I did, I discovered new strength, resilience, and a deeper understanding of what I was capable of. It was a victory over my limitations, which wouldn't have been possible if I had mistaken depletion for defeat.

The next time you find yourself in a trial—whether physical, emotional, or spiritual—ask yourself this: Am I truly *defeated*, or am I just *depleted?* The answer could determine whether you continue to grow or stop short of your full potential.

CHAPTER 8
COST OR PRICE

Price: The upfront, visible amount paid to acquire something, typically measured in money. It's what you see on the tag, the total on the receipt, or the number on the contract. Price is a one-time transaction—tangible, immediate, and often misleading in its simplicity.

Cost: The true toll or impact of a decision, often hidden, ongoing, and more personal than financial. Cost accounts for what you must give up over time: your time, peace, relationships, or potential. It's not just what you pay now—it's what it may require of you later.

"How much is it?" It's a question we ask all the time—at stores, in meetings, or even silently when something catches our eye. It's one of those questions that shows up often in life. But it's almost always focused on **price,** not **cost**. I'll never forget the lesson that helped me understand the difference.

In my second year with Dictaphone Corporation, my first job out of college, as a sales representative selling dictation equipment to doctors and attorneys, I failed in sales. Two years in, I was consistently dead last in national sales rankings. Desperate to turn things around, I asked one of the District Sales Managers to ride along on my calls, hoping he'd throw me a lifeline.

That manager, Charlie, ultimately became one of the most influential mentors in my life. After a long day of sales visits, I noticed a set of cassette tapes in the passenger seat of his car, Zig Ziglar's *See You at the Top* series. When I asked about them, he told me to get my hands on the series and listen to it between every sales call. "Fill your car with this stuff," he said. "Turn it into your university on wheels."

I was pumped. "Can I borrow them?" I asked. He shook his head. "Nope. They're only a hundred bucks. Buy them."

Now, this was back when I could barely justify buying name-brand toilet paper. I told him, "Charlie, I've had two years of bad sales. I can't afford to buy them at that *price*."

That's when he hit me with a sentence that would change my life: "What's the *cost* if you don't?"

It landed like a thunderclap. Like the first time you hear *John 3:16* and realize the depth of God's love for you. That question echoed in my mind, and in many ways, has never stopped.

Everything in life has both a price and a cost. The problem is that we focus so much on the price that we rarely pause to consider the cost. Is it any wonder so many people are buried in debt, living paycheck to paycheck, chasing shiny things without counting what they'll really have to pay?

That one idea—price vs. cost—became the fuel that changed my entire sales career. It even led me to design *nobility selling*, a sales approach where I didn't push a product because of a sales quota, but I truly helped customers understand their needs and make wise, long-term decisions.

Over the years, that mindset led to a successful journey through three distinct sales careers: from Digital Sales Specialist to Cardiovascular Sales Specialist, and ultimately to Vice President of Industrial Electronic Sales. But it all started with an obscure little product and an overlooked feature.

Let me tell you about the Dictaphone. It was the brainchild of Alexander Graham Bell in 1907, created to record

42

sound onto beeswax cylinders using a tiny needle, sort of the great-grandfather of modern voice tech. For decades, doctors and attorneys used cassette-tape Dictaphones to dictate letters and reports. Even in the 1980s and 1990s, they remained a staple in many professional offices.

One feature, in particular, set the Dictaphone apart from all other competitors: VOX, or voice-activated recording. It allowed users to leave the machine on, but it only recorded when someone spoke, cutting out dead air and the need to press buttons constantly. While Dictaphone had mastered instant activation, it's cheaper competitors, such as Radio Shack, had a frustrating delay of a second or two before recording.

Why does that matter? Because one day, as I sat in a doctor's waiting room preparing for a sales meeting, the doctor walked out looking completely distraught. I asked what was wrong, and he explained he'd just been hit with a $250,000 lawsuit. Not for a botched surgery. Not for a bad diagnosis. But for a missing word!

The patient's cancer diagnosis test had come back non-malignant. But the doctor had used a cheap $45 Radio Shack voice recorder. The delayed recording left off the word "non," and all that made it into the transcription was "malignant." That error told a healthy patient they had cancer. The emotional and legal fallout? Massive.

That doctor paid a low **price** for the recorder, but the cost was devastating. As I drove home that day, I couldn't stop thinking: Had he invested in the $415 Dictaphone, that entire nightmare would have been avoided. Immediately, I understood something that no sales training ever taught me: the real *cost* of a cheap purchase choice.

We often use the words' *price*' and '*cost*' interchangeably, but they're not. Understanding the difference changes the way you think. It helps you look past the sticker and consider the whole story—what your choice may cost you over time.

This principle can guide your budget, your investments, even your career choices. It can save your peace, your relationships, and your integrity. In your personal life, this insight makes you a wiser steward. You start asking different questions before making a decision:

- What will this require of me?
- What's the long-term impact?
- Am I buying ease now at the expense of difficulty later?

In business, this mindset helps you sell with integrity. You educate your customers, offer full value, and earn loyalty by helping people make better decisions, not just cheaper ones. You build trust. You build a name that lasts.

But beyond finances and business, this truth goes deeper—it touches legacy. Think of planting a tree. The sapling may cost $25. That's the price. But the cost includes digging the hole, watering it, nurturing it over the years. Yet as it grows, it gives back shade, oxygen, beauty, and a legacy for future generations. It becomes something far more than a transaction. It becomes a symbol of growth, stewardship, and long-term vision. That's the difference between price and cost.

And in the words of my twelve-year-old daughter at the time—after I explained all this at dinner—she looked up and said, "So Daddy, what you're saying is... *price* is a one-time thing, but *cost* is an ongoing thing."

Exactly. And I couldn't have said it better myself.

CHAPTER 9
OUTDATED OR UPDATED

Outdated: A mindset, method, or model that once served a purpose but is now ineffective, unsafe, or irrelevant due to changes in context, needs, or available knowledge.

Updated: The intentional process of improving, adapting, or refining something—whether an idea, system, or behavior—to meet current realities, demands, or understandings.

In this world of innovation and progress, the term "outdated" is a poignant reminder of the perils of clinging to tradition and resisting change. It's not merely a matter of being old-fashioned; it's about the potential consequences of refusing to update and adapt. This chapter delves into the heart of the issue, showcasing that it's not just a generation tug-of-war or the perpetuation of obsolete parental views. It's a journey that emphasizes the importance of embracing those who dare to question the status quo, as long as such questioning emerges from trust, the pursuit of wisdom, and a desire for win-win outcomes.

To illustrate the power of clinging to the old ways, consider the tragic tale of the Titanic, a story familiar to many, yet perhaps not as well understood as one might think. The popular narrative often attributes the ship's demise to a pivotal encounter with an iceberg on that fateful night of April 15th, 1912. The iconic scene in films portrays the "unsinkable" ship encountering the icy grip of the North Atlantic. However, the truth reveals a more complex tale.

The Titanic's collision with an iceberg was pivotal, leading to its eventual sinking over two hours and forty minutes. But, beyond this singular incident lies a compelling case study of the perils of adhering to outdated rules, by resisting safety guideline updates, and the corrosive influence of greed. These factors, more than the iceberg, bore the brunt of responsibility for the tragic loss of nearly 1,500 lives. Blaming an iceberg is a human way of absolving guilt and transferring blame to an inanimate object. It's simpler to point fingers at an object than to accept the harsh reality of human errors and greed.

From its inception, the Titanic was hailed as a legend, a symbol of human achievement. As one of the ship's owners said, it was "designed to be unsinkable, a lifeboat in itself." This statement dripped with ego and hubris, foreshadowing the impending calamity. The original design called for sixty-four lifeboats, a prudent number given the ship's immense size and passenger capacity. However, during the ship's construction, shipowners made a fatal decision to reduce the number of lifeboats to twenty-four life-saving vessels, each capable of accommodating 70 passengers. Their rationale? The abundance of lifeboats would mar the aesthetics of the First-Class deck, obscuring the guests' views. This decision to prioritize aesthetics over passenger safety helped contribute to the loss of 1,514 lives on the Titanic.

In an ironic twist of fate, Alexander Montgomery Carlisle, the director of shipbuilding responsible for ship safety, staunchly opposed this reduction in lifeboat numbers. His recommendations were ignored, ultimately leading to his frustration and retirement. At the heart of this decision was the misguided belief that existing safety regulations, followed for two decades, were sufficient. The prevailing argument asserted that as sea-worthy vessels became safer, there was no need to revisit these rules.

The Titanic saga serves as a poignant reminder that adhering to current rules and regulations is not always sufficient. This historical example reveals the dire consequences of adherence to outdated practices. In the wake of this disaster, the international maritime community swiftly ensured that no soul aboard a ship would be without a spot on a lifeboat should the need to abandon the vessel arise. The International Maritime Committee now enforces strict regulations, mandating a sufficient number of lifeboats to guarantee a seat for every person on board. More than a century ago, the Titanic's demise offered a poignant analogy, illustrating the dire consequences that may arise from neglecting updates and revisions to one's approach.

However, before you join the chorus of criticism aimed at those who stick to outdated practices, it's essential to recognize the potential pitfalls of embracing new ideas and technology. To illustrate, let's delve deeper into the Titanic's story.

Described by the New York Times as "Practically a floating palace," the Titanic stood as an emblem of its era, celebrated as a marvel of technology and a pinnacle of luxury. One of the well-known technological advancements aboard was the remarkable progress made in the domain of radio communication. Implementing the Marconi wireless telegraph on the Titanic marked a pivotal technological advancement during the early 20th century and played a vital role in the ship's communication systems. This cutting-edge telegraph system facilitated ship-to-ship and onshore communications. However, introducing this updated technology, without clear protocols and fueled by unwarranted confidence in its capabilities, would prove to be a direct contributor to the tragic fate of the Titanic.

During the evening, the Titanic received several warnings about the presence of icebergs in its path. These warnings were also obtained by other ships in the area using the new wireless technology. It's generally believed that the Titanic received at least six iceberg warnings. Unfortunately, due to various factors, including a backlog of passenger messages and miscommunication, the ship could not take timely evasive action..

Movie-watchers and the general public might not realize that the individuals responsible for operating the communication systems aboard the Titanic were not part of the ship's crew but were employed by the Marconi Company. Complicating matters further, this technology was primarily leveraged for profit, with the primary duty of the radio operators being the transmission and reception of passenger messages. Distress signals and communications from other vessels had a secondary role. On the tragic night of the disaster, the radio operators found themselves overwhelmed by a substantial backlog of passenger messages, diverting their attention from crucial warnings. Among these ignored messages were those from the nearby SS Californian, whose radio operator, Cyril Evans, diligently attempted to communicate the presence of nearby icebergs through Morse Code messages. These warnings did not receive the attention they warranted, as evidenced by the response from the Titanic's radio operator, Jack Phillips, who tersely stated, "Shut up, shut up, I am busy. I am working the Cape Race."

Bringing a new or updated product to market without establishing clear protocols for its usage can lead to several significant downsides, including safety risks, product misuse, customer confusion, regulatory compliance issues, and even reduced effectiveness.

The stark contrast between *"outdated"* and *"updated"* products or procedures comes to life through the story of the Titanic's ill-fated maiden voyage. It points out the perils of adhering to tradition and resisting change, emphasizing that it's not merely about being old-fashioned but can have catastrophic consequences. The Titanic's sinking reveals a multifaceted tale of human errors, hubris, and profit-driven decisions that had dire consequences. This historical account serves as a saddening analogy, highlighting the necessity of updating and revising practices while cautioning against the pitfalls of embracing new technology without clear protocols. Ultimately, this chapter underscores the delicate balance between tradition and progress, where the pursuit of wisdom and the desire for win-win outcomes should guide the way.

The question we must now confront is this: Have we learned from the Titanic? Or are we simply swapping ocean liners for algorithms, wireless telegraphs for artificial intelligence, while still captained by the same outdated mindsets that once led a ship of dreams to the ocean floor?

Artificial Intelligence is the marvel of our age, the modern embodiment of progress and innovation. Just as the Titanic was seen as the pinnacle of human achievement—a vessel too advanced to fail—AI is often treated with a similar awe. It's viewed as a solution to everything: faster decision-making, more innovative technology and limitless convenience. But as with the Titanic, the real danger isn't the innovation itself—it's the human ego that drives it, the unquestioned confidence we place in it, and the lack of protocols guiding its use.

The Titanic's failure wasn't a failure of technology. It was a failure of humility, preparation, and priorities. The wireless system worked, but no one created systems to ensure that warnings would be acted upon. Lifeboats could have saved everyone, but appearances were prioritized over preparedness. Likewise, today's AI systems are capable of remarkable things—from creating art to predicting disease—but we have to ask: Are we building systems that protect people, or are we prioritizing profit, prestige, and speed?

AI, like the Marconi wireless system, is being implemented at breathtaking speed, often without clear ethical guidelines or thoughtful integration into society. Developers race to push updates. Corporations rush to adopt the newest tools. But who is checking the iceberg warnings? Who is responsible when decisions once made by human beings—judges, teachers, doctors, even spiritual leaders—are increasingly influenced or replaced by machine logic trained on past data but devoid of human wisdom?

Already, we've seen troubling signs:

- Biased algorithms that reinforce societal inequalities.
- AI-generated misinformation spreads faster than it can be corrected.
- Students are relying on AI to complete assignments before learning the lesson.
- Corporations are replacing entire departments with code, leaving ethics and empathy behind.

In each case, the technology works; it is the *application* that fails. Or, more truthfully, it is the *intentions behind the application* that fail. Just as the Titanic's operators prioritized profits over safety, today's decision-makers may be tempted to use AI not for human flourishing, but for efficiency at the expense of accountability, speed over wisdom, and power over people.

This is why *being updated* isn't just about using the latest tools—it's about upgrading our mindsets, values, and perspectives.

The Titanic taught us that regulations written for one era won't protect us in another. That lesson still applies. As AI reshapes education, employment, relationships, and even our own identities, we must ask:

- What lifeboats are we building into this technology?
- Who's responsible when things go wrong?
- What messages are we ignoring because we're too busy chasing efficiency?

We stand at a similar crossroads—do we arrogantly charge forward, assuming the unsinkability of our creations? Or do we pause long enough to examine whether our values have kept pace with the tools we use?

In the wake of the Titanic's sinking, maritime law underwent significant changes. Lifeboats became mandatory for all. Emergency drills were standardized. Communication protocols were revised. It took a disaster for reform to happen. Will it take a similar moment for us to reconsider how we deploy AI?

Let us not wait for a digital iceberg to awaken our discernment. Let us update not just our software, but our souls. Let us design lifeboats of accountability, wisdom, and humility—so that this time, innovation does not outpace integrity.

CHAPTER 10
INSPIRATION OR MOTIVATION

Inspiration: The spark—it often comes from outside of you. It's what moves your heart, captures your imagination, and fills you with fresh ideas or a sense of purpose. It's often momentary and emotional.

Motivation: The fuel—it's what keeps you moving once the spark fades. It can come from external rewards (like money, praise, or pressure), but the strongest form is intrinsic—when you act from your own desires, goals, or convictions. It's not just a feeling; it's a force.

Are you familiar with the story of a kingdom far, far away, where a remarkably wealthy king lived with a very big dilemma? Though full of kindness and grace, his eldest daughter was not blessed with the beauty that the kingdom's folk admired. In his misguided enthusiasm to find a suitable suitor for her, the king devised a plan that would soon become a legendary tale.

With great fanfare, the king dispatched royal messengers to spread the word throughout his vast realm. Letters were sent to all young men, inviting them to the royal castle on a momentous day. The purpose? To present his unsightly daughter's hand in marriage to the worthiest subject who could prove his courage. On the appointed day, the castle's beautiful courtyard was filled with hopeful young men, each eager to showcase their bravery. The king stood before them, a regal figure of authority, ready to test their mettle. Full of hope, the king revealed a unique challenge, a test of courage and desire. He had a colossal, Olympic-size pool in his courtyard, and within it lurked alligators, piranhas, and venomous water moccasins. The king addressed the assembled men alongside the pool, speaking about the qualities he sought in his future son-in-law. Then, he made an offer to the brave souls who had gathered. For the first young man to swim across the pool and reach the other side, a choice among three prizes would be granted: a lifetime supply of food for himself and his family, a cozy cottage for his family with five fertile acres of land for farming, or the hand of his daughter in marriage and the boundless wealth of his kingdom.

No sooner did the king finish speaking than a great splash echoed through the courtyard, followed by a young man catapulting himself out of the far side of the dangerous pool in record time. The king was astounded by the man's incredible athletic prowess and undaunted enthusiasm. Approaching the young hero, the king exclaimed, "I have never witnessed such unbridled determination, young man! Tell me, is it the lifetime of sustenance for you and your family that you desire?" The young man shook his head and replied, "No, sire." "Perhaps the charming cottage and fertile land?" the king inquired. Again, the young man declined, "No, sire." The king joyously said, "Well, it must be my daughter's hand in marriage and all the wealth of my kingdom?" But once more, the young man answered, "No, sire." The king, his confusion growing, asked, "Young man, I do not understand what it is you want?" With sheer determination, the young man responded, "I want the name of the fool who pushed me into the pool!"

Sometimes, through the eyes of our enthusiasm, we mistake the origins of other people's motivation.

I will never forget the first time one of my sales representatives approached me, requesting an increase in his sales commission plan. This request followed three consecutive months of failing to meet his sales targets. The salesperson attributed his lack of motivation to the commission structure, which, he believed, hindered his ability to sell our services effectively. Despite numerous coaching sessions to bolster his efforts, I grew increasingly frustrated with his lack of improvement. As a final, desperate measure, I granted his request, raising his commission rate by five percent. As it turned out, this decision proved to be a significant mistake, but it also became a valuable life lesson.

Motivation is a dual-sided coin; it's a lifelong journey we must continually travel. The key lies in approaching this journey with the proper perspective, or you will be perpetually out of breath and disheartened. On one side of the motivational coin lies the question, "How can I motivate myself to…?" Conversely, we find the question, "How can I motivate others to…?"

This chapter delves into the latter question and brace yourself for a potentially surprising perspective. Contrary to conventional wisdom, my stance as a motivational speaker may astonish you: "You *can't* motivate others!" Before you object, take a moment and pause. I'm not physically present, but I can sense the tension and defensiveness that might be welling up within you. The instinct to argue, "Of course you can!" is natural. I know this because I spent years convincing my mentor that my passion and enthusiasm were infectious enough to motivate others to become as disciplined as I am in achieving goals. However, my experiences, much like the anecdote about the sales representative, led me to a different conclusion. Let me clarify, you can induce short-term actions in others through positive or negative means, but you cannot instigate lasting behavioral changes. Consider this example: I could instruct an employee that failing to make ten additional sales calls daily to improve their sales performance will result in their termination. Fearing job loss, they might comply for a day, maybe two, or even a week- just long enough to update their resume and seek alternative employment.

As the sales representative demonstrated, effectiveness can be negligible even when employing a more positive approach. As the reader, you might argue that a more significant commission increase would have been more motivating. Perhaps initially, but how sustainable would that motivation be after facing multiple rejections?

Let's burrow deeper into this newly recognized truth. Consider seminars you've participated in, whether organized by your workplace, educational institution, or related to your favorite interest. How much knowledge acquired from participating in these sessions is actively integrated into your daily life today? Have you ever wondered why successful individuals readily share their success techniques and do not fear losing their status to those they mentor? It's because they recognize that only a select few genuinely put into practice what they've learned beyond the initial enthusiasm of the seminar. Most attendees don't open their information binders after leaving the seminar room. Inspiring people for a few hours or even a weekend is relatively simple. But their inspiration dissipates rapidly as soon as they leave the immediate influence.

Motivation closely resembles the sales process. Those who struggle in sales are often under the impression that the industry revolves around "convincing" or "manipulating" others into buying their products or services. This couldn't be further from reality. While such *tactics* (reread Chapter 1) might yield a few sales in the short term, they are typically followed by "buyer's remorse." A successful salesperson understands that selling is defined as a "transference of passion." It's impossible to change someone's mind. No one can alter another person's beliefs on their behalf. Instead, one can offer additional information for them to consider, and it is ultimately their choice whether this supplementary information is compelling enough to reshape their beliefs or perspective. Motivation operates on a similar principle. It's the transfer of passion rooted in inspiration, willingly embraced and harnessed as an internal, ongoing force that drives one to pursue their full potential.

Consider the analogy of motivation being akin to fuel for a car's engine; motivation is the internal force that propels you to act and attain goals. Much like gasoline or an energy source in a car engine, motivation is the energy that moves you forward. However, this internal force remains dormant until embraced and channeled, just as fuel is useless to a vehicle until it's inside the gas tank. Moreover, the engine may require a specific fuel type, akin to motivation, aligning with personal values and aspirations for optimal performance. Using the wrong kind of fuel, just as failing to align motivation with personal values and goals, can result in inefficient progress.

On the other hand, inspiration is the spark plug in a car engine, initiating the process. The catalyst ignites the engine, like the spark that ignites the fuel-air mixture and starts combustion in a car engine. Inspiration is the initial spark or idea that kickstarts motivation, providing the fuel to pursue specific goals or dreams.

You can even add aspiration to this analogy as the destination or goal you aim to reach with your "motivation-fueled car." Aspirations provide a clear purpose and direction for your motivation and inspiration, much like a destination guides a car's journey. Your aspirations define where you want to go, be it a specific location or a desired outcome, and guide your motivation and inspiration toward a unified and sustainable path to success. Just as a car's journey benefits from a well-defined destination, motivation and inspiration thrive when aligned with clear, personally meaningful aspirations.

I hope you're beginning to see that motivating others by offering rewards or encouraging them externally doesn't really work over the long run. Failing to grasp this, you could spend a significant amount of your time and energy on people who aren't internally motivated. This would mean you're missing out on helping someone who is eager to learn from you and is internally encouraged to apply what you teach.

When mentors misinterpret what their mentees genuinely want, they are tempted to offer more external rewards, such as increasing a commission rate or using positive reinforcement. The mentor might become even more frustrated when these efforts fail to yield significant results, and they may invest even more resources in trying to salvage the mentoring relationship. Mentors should determine what drives the mentee from the inside, working together to discover and nurture those inner forces. The mentor's role shifts from trying to force motivation from the outside to creating an environment where the mentee's internal motivation can flourish. It is essential to be willing to accept when the mentee is not responding positively and to permit yourself to step away without feeling guilty, if not for any other reason than to maintain an optimal level of internal motivation.

Interestingly, the sales rep did not improve his performance even after receiving a raise. Surprisingly, he wasn't satisfied with the raise and asked for more. My response to him was, "Your raise will be effective when you are!"

If you want to learn more about what motivates people, Daniel H. Pink's <u>Drive: The Surprising Truth About What Motivates Us</u> is a great book. Based on research from various fields, this discussion explores the nature of motivation and suggests that everyone is driven by "mastery, autonomy, and purpose." The book changed how I utilize my time and energy to harness the internal motivation of others effectively.

CHAPTER 11
AWARDS OR REWARDS

Awards: A visible, external recognition given by others, often based on a specific performance, competition, or standard of excellence. It is usually a result of judgment, evaluation, or comparison.

Rewards: A deeper, often internal benefit gained through effort, growth, or meaningful contribution. It may or may not come with public recognition, but it leaves a lasting impact on your character, values, and life experience.

The adult Sunday School class erupted in laughter as the dirty Santa gift was pulled from the Christmas bag. Michael Angelo's famous sculpture of *David* immediately came to mind as everyone gasped at the eighteen-inch bronze bodybuilder trophy for first place. The red ribbon tied around the statue's neck only heightened the hilarity and desirability of the gift, which was promptly stolen three times before being taken out of the dirty Santa game, as per the game's rules.

Ironically, this trophy hadn't been admired like that since the day it was awarded to me many years ago, during my competitive years in natural bodybuilding competitions. In recent years, it had been gathering dust, along with the rest of my old trophies, up in our attic.

My wife and I rediscovered the trophy while cleaning the attic one evening. As we dug through the old boxes, we began discussing why these trophies no longer held the same meaning as they once did. Something that had once represented an emotional high now signified little more than a distant memory. Our conversation deepened as we wondered why some trophies were on display in our home while most were hidden away in the dark corners of the attic. Our conversation revealed that the trophies on display had nothing to do with their beauty, size, or even the achieved placement they represented. The awards we had chosen to display in plain sight were linked to a deeper meaning—they all began with a story of failure or struggle. Ultimately, we realized the gratification came from the stories and memories they represented, the journey of overcoming trials, setbacks, and obstacles. The real reward was not in the trophy we received but in the lessons we learned and the character we built along the way.

My martial arts school participates in many tournaments each year. Mr. McCall typically provides t-shirts for our students to wear to represent our dojo. Regardless of the logo he chooses to be on the t-shirt, the following words are always printed – "Win or Learn." This is not just a cute slogan. The results we seek from our students who participate are winning and learning. We put an equal value on both outcomes. Very often, we celebrate a student who learned a valuable growth lesson just as much as one who may have earned first place. A lesson learned has a more significant impact over the long run than a shiny trophy.

It's time we reframe what success and significance look like and the efforts we pour into achieving them (Read Chapter Three). We are taught to strive to be number one from an early age: to get straight A's in school, to be the team captain, etc. But we have little or no contemplation of the value of the journey itself. When we receive a school report card, we quickly focus on next semester's grades. The day after we cross the finish line, we are already thinking about the next race. We focus on the next opponent as soon as we finish playing the game.

I am reminded of a valuable lesson a close friend shared as he realized he was always looking for the next adventure and often missed out on experiencing the journey he was already on.

As a reward for working so hard to lose the extra thirty pounds of weight he had put on over the years, Wayne dreamed of reaching the summit of Clingman's Dome, the highest point in North Carolina. He had heard of the breathtaking view from the observation tower, where, on a clear day, you could see as many as seven states – North Carolina, Tennessee, South Carolina, Georgia, Kentucky, Virginia, and even Alabama.

He prepared meticulously for the hike, driven by the idea of standing at the top and seeing the world from such a lofty vantage point. Along the way, he met many hikers, all with the same goal in mind. Some chatted about the beautiful wildflowers, the ancient trees, and the peacefulness of the Smokey Mountains. But Wayne wasn't interested in the journey; he was fixated on one thing – the view from the summit, the ultimate award.

He hiked briskly, passing others on the trail, his eyes set on the prize. He finally had his moment when he reached the observation tower at the top of Clingman's Dome. The sky was crystal clear, and the view stretched out in every direction. Wayne could see seven states – each one a distinct patchwork of rolling hills and valleys, shimmering rivers, and distant mountain ranges. He snapped photos, imagining how many likes and comments his friends would give him for his remarkable achievement. But as he stood at the top, something unexpected happened. Instead of soaking in the beauty of the moment, Wayne found his gaze wandering to the distant mountain range beyond. Mount LeConte was in Tennessee, standing tall in the distance and beyond that, the Blue Ridge Mountains. He began to wonder what the view might be like from those peaks. Were they taller? Did they offer something more spectacular than Clingman's Dome? And what about the mountains in Georgia, Kentucky, and Virginia? Were their summits more challenging to reach?

As his mind raced with curiosity about the other mountain tops, Wayne realized he wasn't even appreciating the view he had worked so hard to see. His thoughts had already shifted to the next summit, the next climb, the next award. The excitement he had felt moments earlier began to fade, replaced by a sense of dissatisfaction. He had reached the top, but now he wondered if something greater was just beyond his grasp.

Wayne's story serves as a reminder to set goals that align with personal values and long-term vision rather than chasing the thrill of recognition. Achieving a milestone is indeed a moment worth celebrating, but what gives it depth and lasting fulfillment is the purpose behind it. Setting goals grounded in personal values enables you to find meaning in the daily grind, even when the applause fades. These goals are not about impressing others but about living authentically and honoring your true priorities. For example, someone who aims to improve their health by exercising may initially be motivated by the desire to look good. However, suppose they come to value the increased energy, mental clarity, and overall well-being they gain from a healthy lifestyle. In that case, they will find the rewards far more fulfilling than simply reaching a target weight.

When we focus on purpose over praise, the rewards often come unexpectedly, during quiet moments of reflection or while overcoming challenges. Growth happens when you look back and see how much you've evolved, realizing that the obstacles you once saw as roadblocks were actually steppingstones to a stronger character. The true rewards lie in the resilience built, the skills acquired, and the relationships formed along the way. It is in the less visible victories, rather than the end result, that the real treasures are found.

Millennials are often ridiculed for rejecting conventional paths to success, but they may be onto something. This generation has placed a higher emphasis on impact over recognition, questioning whether titles, corner offices, or gold watches truly equate to a meaningful life. Instead of chasing positions of prestige, they seek work that aligns with their purpose, even if it means foregoing traditional markers of success. For example, many choose jobs with lower pay if it allows them to contribute to causes they care about, or they prioritize work-life balance over climbing the corporate ladder. They recognize that true rewards come from knowing they've made a difference, not from having their name engraved on a plaque.

As you consider your own path, challenge yourself to think about the impact you're making on others. Are your goals driven by the need for external validation, or are they guided by a deeper desire to leave a positive imprint on the world? How do your actions influence the lives of those around you? Strive for goals that lead not just to applause but to a legacy of change long after the spotlight has dimmed.

Understanding the difference between "awards" and "rewards" is crucial. Awards are tangible symbols of achievement—recognition from others that you've reached a certain standard. Rewards, however, are often intangible and come from within, rooted in personal growth, the satisfaction of hard work, and the joy of making a meaningful difference. When we pursue rewards over awards, we focus on significance rather than success, on the journey rather than the destination. It's in these moments of true reflection that we realize the real prize isn't a trophy but the person we've become along the way.

Fortunately for Wayne, unlike many of us, he realized that his eyes were on the wrong prize. He used his mountain-top experience and sat off to the side for some solitude and reflection as he breathed in the majestic views from the observation tower. To learn from this experience and capitalize on his newfound wisdom, he set a new goal emphasizing the journey rather than the destination. An *award* can signify the end of an achievement, but the *reward* is in the ongoing transformation that occurs because of the effort invested.

CHAPTER 12
BITTER OR BETTER

Bitter: A hardened emotional state marked by unresolved pain, resentment, or cynicism caused by disappointment, loss, or perceived injustice. Bitterness quietly poisons perspective, keeping wounds open and preventing growth.

Better: A deliberate choice to grow through pain, not just go through it. To become stronger, wiser, and more compassionate as a result of hardship. "Better" doesn't erase the struggle — it reclaims it with purpose.

If you are reading this, chances are life hasn't been easy lately. Perhaps you've been navigating the loss of a loved one, juggling the relentless demands of work and family, or enduring a situation that seems to drain your energy without offering a way out. Life's struggles are real, and they're often overwhelming. It's natural to feel tired, defeated, or even resentful. Yet, in these moments, when life feels heavy and hope seems out of reach, we're faced with one of the most significant choices we can make: the choice to either let life's hardships harden us or to allow them to shape us into someone stronger, wiser, and more compassionate.

This choice doesn't deny the reality of your pain. It doesn't demand that you "Look on the bright side" or minimize your suffering. Instead, it offers a powerful truth: you may not have control over what happens to you, but you do have control over how you respond. Each morning, you may be used to an alarm clock awakening you. Why not set an opportunity clock? No one wants to be alarmed first thing in the morning. Each morning is an invitation – a fork in the road. Will you let bitterness take the wheel, or will you embrace the courage to be better despite it all?

This choice, though empowering, isn't as simple as flipping a switch. If it were, we'd all live in perpetual peace and positivity. But the reality is that our minds are not always our allies. In fact, the thoughts that dominate our minds can feel like unwelcome house guests who've overstayed their welcome.

A 2020 study from Queen's University found that the average person has around 6,200 thoughts per day. Astoundingly, about 80% of these thoughts tend to be negative. Think about that for a moment: before first sip of coffee, your brain is already teeming with self-doubt, worry, or even criticism.

This negativity isn't entirely your fault. It's rooted in our biology – a survival mechanism hardwired into our brains to alert us to danger. But while this instinct may have been helpful when our ancestors faced saber-toothed tigers, it's less valuable when dealing with modern-day struggles like a demanding boss, a broken relationship, or financial stress.

Here's the catch: negativity may be our default setting, but it doesn't have to be our destiny. The thoughts that pass through our minds don't have to define us. Instead, we can challenge them, reframe them, and redirect them. To understand the power of this choice, consider Viktor Frankl, a Holocaust survivor whose life was a testament to the resilience of the human spirit. Frankl endured the unimaginable – years in Nazi concentration camps, where loss, hunger, and despair were constants. He was stripped of everything: his family, his freedom, and even the promise of a future.

And yet, amidst this horror, Frankl discovered something extraordinary. While he couldn't control his circumstances, he realized he could control one thing: his response to them. In his book, <u>Man's Search for Meaning</u>, Frankl wrote, "Everything can be taken from a man but one thing: the last of the human freedoms – to choose one's attitude in any given set of circumstances, to choose one's own way."

Frankl's insight doesn't minimize the reality of pain; rather, it illuminates a profound truth: our circumstances, no matter how grim, cannot dictate our lives unless we allow them to. His story reminds us that we retain the power to choose even in the darkest moments.

Frankl's philosophy is inspiring, but how do we apply it in our lives? How do we choose to be "better" instead of bitter? One of the most accessible and effective tools we all carry is gratitude. Practicing gratitude isn't just a feel-good exercise; it has a measurable impact on the brain. Studies show that gratitude activates the prefrontal cortex (responsible for decision-making) and the anterior cingulate cortex (which regulates emotions). Over time, rewiring of the brain helps foster a more optimistic outlook.

But there's more. Gratitude also triggers the release of dopamine and serotonin, the "feel-good" chemicals that improve mood and enhance resilience. Regularly practicing gratitude can reshape your brain, helping you become more resilient in the face of challenges.

How can you start? Each morning, take a moment to write down three things for which you're grateful. Be specific. Don't just write, "I'm grateful for my family." Instead, write, "I'm grateful for the hug my daughter gave me yesterday when I felt overwhelmed." This simple practice might feel insignificant at first, but over time, it has the power to shift your perspective.

Imagine your mind as a garden. If left untended, weeds – negative thoughts – will take over. But if you're intentionally planting seeds of gratitude, hope, and resilience, you can cultivate a space where growth flourishes. This isn't about achieving perfection. Some days, bitterness will feel like the easier choice. And that's okay. Progress, not perfection, is the goal. Choosing better is about taking one small step each day toward growth, whether it's practicing gratitude, reframing a negative thought, or simply pausing to breathe deeply when you feel overwhelmed.

Choosing to be better doesn't just transform your life; it impacts those around you. You become a light source in a dark world when you choose gratitude over grumbling, hope over despair, and resilience over defeat. Your decision to rise above bitterness inspires others to do the same. Think of a pebble dropped into a still pond. The ripples spread outward, touching every corner of the water. Your choice to be better is that pebble. The ripples it creates – your kindness, strength, and courage – can touch lives in ways you may never fully see.

As you consider the thousands of thoughts you'll have today, remember this: you don't have to let negativity dominate. Each thought is an opportunity to redirect your mind toward hope and resilience. The result won't be a perfect life, but it will be a life of progress – a life that, despite hardships, is rich with meaning and growth. Bitterness may seem justified in the face of life's challenges, but it will rob you of joy, peace, and purpose. Choosing better, on the other hand, allows you to face life with strength and grace. So today, and every day, the choice is yours. Will you let life's challenges embitter you, or will you rise with the courage to become better? Is today "day one," or will it be just another, "one day..."

CHAPTER 13
FRUITS OR ROOTS

Fruit: The visible results of effort — achievements, rewards, recognition, or success that come after a season of growth. They're what others see, celebrate, and often desire, but they are temporary and seasonal.

Roots: The unseen foundation that supports lasting growth — values, disciplines, beliefs, and relationships that nourish and sustain you through every season. They determine your ability to endure challenges and continue growing, even when no fruit is visible.

Imagine standing in your backyard, gazing at a magnificent apple tree. Its branches are heavy with vibrant, shiny fruit. Most people would focus on the apples – they're sweet, visible, and the ultimate reward of the tree's growth. But what they can't see and often neglect is the tree's secret to thriving: its deep, strong roots. In our fast-paced lives, it is so easy to see things for face value and completely miss out on the rich rewards offered when we look a little deeper. Sure, picking the ripe and delicious apple provides immediate satisfaction to our taste pallet, but by giving some attention to the roots, we can nourish our bodies for life. The old saying goes, "Deep and strong roots never see the frost."

In our fast-paced world, the appeal of quick rewards and instant wins is undeniable. Social media platforms reward us with likes and comments in seconds. Online shopping offers same-day delivery. The phrase "Buy now, pay later" has become a mantra for modern living. These immediate rewards trigger a surge of dopamine, the brain's chemical messenger of pleasure, and this drive for instant gratification is hardwired into us. Scientists call this *temporal discounting*, where we prioritize smaller, immediate rewards over greater, future ones. Studies show that when faced with a choice between $50 now or $100 a year later, many people choose the smaller, immediate reward, even if the long-term gains are significantly greater. This bias is driven by the brain's limbic system, which governs our emotional and impulsive responses, often overpowering the rational prefrontal cortex that helps us weigh long-term benefits.

While the fruits of life are enticing, they cannot sustain us through life's challenges. The frost – symbolizing setbacks, failures, and hardships – will inevitably come. When it does, only deep roots can keep us grounded. Roots represent the foundations we build over time: our core values, relationships, habits, and spiritual practices. Unlike the fleeting pleasure of fruits, roots provide lasting fulfillment and resilience. Consider a tree with shallow roots; it might produce fruit for a season but will topple in the first strong wind. By contrast, a tree with deep roots not only survives but thrives through every season.

The story of the Malaysian bamboo beautifully illustrates this principle. When the bamboo is planted, it requires years of daily care – watering, fertilizing, and tending to the soil – with no visible growth above the surface. There has been nothing to show for the effort for five years, but during this time, the bamboo has grown an extensive underground root system. Then, almost miraculously, the bamboo shoots up nearly ninety feet in a single month. The bamboo's astounding growth is only possible because of the foundation laid during those unseen years. In the same way, our lives require a commitment to cultivating roots – even when progress isn't immediately visible – to experience extraordinary growth later.

Life's frost comes in many forms: job loss, illness, broken relationships, or unmet goals. These moments test the strength of our roots. Without a strong foundation, we're left vulnerable, like a tree with shallow roots in a storm. Angela Duckworth, author of <u>Grit,</u> emphasizes that long-term success comes not from fleeting moments of inspiration but from sustained effort and perseverance. This grit is the product of deep roots – habits, values, and a clear sense of purpose – that enable us to endure and grow through adversity.

The famous Stanford Marshmallow Experiment sheds light on the power of delayed gratification. In this study, children were offered a choice: eat one marshmallow now or wait 15 minutes and receive two marshmallows. Researchers followed these children for decades and found that those who resisted the immediate reward tended to have better life outcomes – higher academic achievement, better health, and greater emotional well-being. This study highlights a critical truth: the ability to delay gratification is a predictor of long-term success. Yet, resisting the pull of immediate rewards is easier said than done. Modern technology and consumer culture amplify the allure of fruits, making it harder than ever to focus on cultivating roots.

Breaking free from the cycle of instant gratification requires intentional action. Identifying core values can serve as a compass in decision-making, while building meaningful habits helps align daily actions with long-term goals. Strengthening relationships provides the support needed to weather life's storms. Mindfulness techniques like meditation can reduce impulsivity and strengthen one's ability to delay gratification. Visualizing long-term rewards, such as a fulfilling career, lasting relationships, and inner peace, can provide motivation to stay grounded.

Let's be clear. This is not a matter of choosing between fruits and roots – it's not an "either/or" dilemma, but rather an "and/but" scenario. Behavioral growth doesn't demand sacrificing one for the other. Instead, wisdom lies in recognizing that you can enjoy the fruits of your labor while remaining deeply rooted in your values and long-term goals. The key is moderation and proportionality: savoring rewards without losing focus on cultivating the foundation that sustains them. By maintaining proportionality, you can achieve both present satisfaction and enduring success.

When we prioritize roots over fruits, we create a life of stability and purpose. The fruits may take longer to appear, but they will be sweeter and more enduring. Reflecting on your life, it's worth asking: Are you chasing fruits or cultivating roots? The frost will come, but with deep, strong roots, you can stand firm and grow taller through every season.

Remember the image of the apple tree, abundant and grounded. Let it remind you that while *fruits* may capture the eye and the stomach, the *roots* sustain the soul. And like the Malaysian bamboo, remember that the unseen, patient work beneath the surface is what enables extraordinary growth. As the saying goes, "Deep, strong roots never see the frost." Choose to nurture your *roots* and moderate your *fruits*.

CHAPTER 14
COMPLAINING OR TRAINING

Complaining: *The act of focusing on what you lack, blaming others or circumstances, and remaining stuck in a cycle of negativity instead of pursuing growth.*

Training: *The intentional process of developing your strengths, confronting your weaknesses, and leveraging every opportunity to become better, regardless of how you feel or what challenges stand in your way.*

Out in the wild, the jungle isn't fair. It never promised to be. Strength doesn't guarantee survival. Speed doesn't guarantee dominance. Looks don't guarantee power. The jungle doesn't care about your resume' – it rewards the ones who adapt, who endure, who learn.

That's why the lion is king. It's not because he's the fastest. He's not. The cheetah will outrun him every time.

It's not because he's the biggest. He's not. The elephant towers over him.

It's not because he's the strongest. He's not. The gorilla could easily outmuscle him.

And it's not because he's the most terrifying-looking. The crocodile owns that title.

So, what makes the lion the king? The lion wins not because of one dominant trait, but because he refuses to lean on just one. He trains. He sharpens every part of himself, his strategy, his stamina, his cunning, his instincts. He doesn't complain about not being the fastest. He doesn't sulk because he's not the biggest. He leverages everything he *is* instead of whining about what he's not. That's what crowns a king.

The world will lie to you and say that second place doesn't matter. That if you're not the best, you're irrelevant. But truthfully, consistency, adaptability, humility and the willingness to train across all areas matter more than being a one-hit wonder. The lion may not win every category, but he shows up in *every* category – and that's what gives him the throne.

So, the question is, "Are you training with what you've been given? Or are you complaining about what you're not?

They were both born with speed in their veins. Both were gifted with once-in-a-generation talent. Both were destined, it seemed, to be the next great name in track and field. But what set them apart wasn't their stride; it was their mindset. One of these two had to RESET their mindset after experiencing failure.

In 2004, a tall, lanky 17-year-old Jamaican named Usain Bolt stepped onto the Olympic stage in Athens. All eyes were on him. Well, sort of. He didn't make it past the first round of his race. A hamstring injury knocked him out early, and critics quickly dismissed him as a fragile sprinter with hype but no hardware. It would have been easy for Bolt to hide behind excuses. Blame the injury. Point fingers. Talk big. Even quit. But he didn't. Instead, he trained. Not just harder, but smarter. He hired new coaches. Adjusted his stride. Focused on form. Strengthened his body. Sharpened his mind. And four years later in Beijing, he didn't just win, he rewrote history. Three gold medals. Three world records. And the start of a legacy that would redefine sprinting. Bolt turned failure into fuel.

In 2021, Sha'Carri Richardson became an overnight sensation. With flaming red hair and raw emotion, she sprinted across the finish line at the U.S. Olympic Trials, earning her a spot as America's next track queen. Cameras captured her joy. Fans embraced her fire. But days later, headlines told a different story: a failed drug test for marijuana meant her Olympic dream was over before it began.

What followed was heartbreaking, not because of the failure, but because of the response. Instead of training through the trial, she leaned into frustration. Her interviews were filled with defiance. Her return to the track wasn't marked by redemption; it was marked by a last-place finish at the Prefontaine Classic. The potential was there, but the focus had shifted. Excuses, not execution. Pain, but no plan. To her credit, in the years since, Sha'Carri has begun to shift. Her growth is evident. But in that critical moment, her reaction stood in stark contrast to Bolt's.

Two athletes. Same sport. Same dream. Both faced setbacks. One trained. One complained.

We all get the same size suitcase: 24 hours. But not everyone packs it with the same purpose. Some stuff it with fluff—scrolls, distractions, petty arguments, and passive waiting. Others fold in reps, reflection, study, and grit. It's not about having more time. It's about what you *do* with that time.

That's the lesson the jungle teaches. It doesn't offer participation trophies. It doesn't care about intentions. It rewards the ones who act—who adapt with urgency and discipline.

Time, like the jungle, is ruthless. It doesn't stretch to accommodate your feelings. It doesn't pause while you figure things out. Time, like a lion's environment, demands respect. You don't get to control the terrain, but you can control your preparation. You can decide whether to pack your suitcase with training or complaining.

The lion doesn't get a head start. He just doesn't waste time wishing he were someone else. He takes inventory, then he gets to work. *That's* the game changer.
The same goes for us.

Maybe you're not the fastest in the room. Maybe you're not the most talented. So what? Pack your suitcase with what you *do* have—discipline, consistency, strategy, humility. It's not about being born to dominate. It's about choosing to show up every single day with intention.
Usain Bolt failed on the world's biggest stage. But he didn't throw his suitcase out the window. He reorganized it. Traded hype for hunger. Turned pain into purpose. By the time Beijing came around, he didn't need to prove he was the fastest—he had *trained* to be undeniable.

Sha'Carri? She had the same fire. The same chance. The same suitcase. But her initial reaction was to dump it out in frustration. Instead of repacking it with clarity and conviction, she filled it with noise. And that's what slowed her down—not talent, but turmoil. Thankfully, she's begun to reclaim her focus, proving it's never too late to reset your mindset. But the lesson remains: potential is never enough. It's how you pack the suitcase.

Here's the truth: In the moments we are being challenged, we do not rise to the occasion; we fall to the level of our training. The world is going to hand you the same 24 hours whether you're on top of your game or flat on your back. You can use that time to train, to adapt, to grow—or you can waste it explaining why you're not further along. You don't need more hours. You need more *ownership*.
So ask yourself today—are you living like a king in the jungle of your calling? Or are you standing on the edge of the wild, suitcase in hand, waiting for life to feel fair?

CHAPTER 15
SEES POSSIBILITIES OR SEIZE POSSIBILITIES

Sees: To perceive with the eyes or to recognize mentally; to observe or become aware of something as it exists. In the context of mindset, "seeing" is the act of identifying a problem, challenge, or opportunity— but without necessarily engaging it.

Seize: To take hold of suddenly or forcibly; to grasp mentally and act decisively upon an opportunity. In the context of mindset, "seizing" is the intentional action of stepping into responsibility, taking initiative, and owning the process of creating change.

On a cold January evening, I found myself once again wrapped up in one of life's most *delightful* experiences: shopping for a car. Yes, I'm being sarcastic. I was two weeks deep into spending every evening researching, evaluating, and comparing prices, all in preparation for the exhausting, drawn-out dance we call "negotiating."

Now, I know this dance well—not because I'm light on my feet, but because early in my career, I invented a car-buying product for people with C and D credit ratings while working for Dictaphone Corporation. That experience taught me just how flawed and frustrating the process can be for novice car buyers.

Apparently, my wife had reached her breaking point after being within earshot of my nightly grumbling for far too long. Sitting beside me on our long red sofa, she finally spewed, "Would you just go buy the damn car?" Startled, I looked at her and said, "This is absolutely ridiculous. I'm the one spending $20,000 to $30,000 on a new car, and *I'm* the one doing all the work? I should be able to simply shout out to the world, 'Hey, I want to buy this particular car, and then let *them* come to *me*, making offers and competing for my business."

And that's when it hit me: Why hasn't someone invented a reverse car-buying auction?

This was in 2011, just before mobile apps really took off, and around the time when e-commerce was finally becoming more trusted. The U.S. was still emerging from the 2008 financial crisis—unemployment remained high, people were struggling to find steady employment, and policymakers were debating how best to revive the economy: through more government spending or deeper budget cuts?

Despite the uncertainty, a growing national focus on innovation and entrepreneurship emerged. People were hungry for fresh ideas and new solutions. Shows like *Shark Tank* were just starting to capture the imagination of would-be entrepreneurs, and the small business boom was gaining momentum.

That's when I discovered an entrepreneurial contest hosted by the Chamber of Commerce for the "Best New Idea" to bring to market. For me, this was the moment I moved from being "problem-focused" to "solution-oriented." Though I wrestled with whether I could afford the $100 entry fee, knowing we had a two-year-old still in diapers, I chose to seize the opportunity. I was going to design, create, and implement the first "website-based car-buying solution that would match "ready-to-purchase" car buyers with auto-retailers in a confidential and secure manner, shifting the feelings of power and control to the car buyer."

It's interesting how inspiration can arise from frustration. That night, it wasn't a lightning bolt of genius that struck me—it was irritation, impatience, and my wife's blunt honesty that lit the fuse. But here's the catch: most people live in that moment every day. They see what's wrong. They talk about what's broken. They vent, post, complain, analyze, and repeat. But few *act* on a solution. Why? Because seeing the possibility gives us the illusion of progress. It tricks our brains into thinking we're "on the path" when in reality, we're just standing at the trailhead taking selfies.

Let me be clear: seeing isn't bad. In fact, seeing is essential. You can't fix what you don't acknowledge. But if all you ever do is *see* the problem, you're like the guy standing next to a house fire shouting, "Hey, everyone! That house is on fire!" while holding a bucket of water and refusing to throw it.

There comes a time in every person's life when you have to decide if you're going to be a spectator or a participant. A critic or a creator. Someone who complains about how broken the system is—or someone who says, "I may not have all the answers, but I'm willing to be part of the solution.

That $100 contest entry fee might not sound like a big deal to some, but at that point in my life, it was a risk. It was a diaper gamble. It meant choosing belief over doubt, progress over perfection, and courage over comfort.

And you know what? That decision changed everything. Not just because of what came out of it (we'll get to that later), but because of what it *activated* in me. I stopped being someone who saw problems and started becoming someone who seized possibilities.

Let me pause and ask you a tricky question: What's something you've been staring at for too long, waiting for the "right time" to act?

- Is it a business idea?
- Is it a conversation you know you need to have?

- Is it a life pattern that you recognize as unhealthy?
- Is it a gap in your church, community, or industry that you keep pointing out?

Here's the truth: the longer you wait to "seize," the stronger the fear becomes. The window doesn't always stay open. Eventually, your great idea becomes someone else's breakthrough because they are willing to act while you are still evaluating.

There have been times when I chose to seize the opportunity, and things didn't turn out the way I hoped. But every time I acted, I walked away with something far more valuable than regret: growth. Even the so-called "failures" taught me lessons that success couldn't. In the case of my reverse auto-auction idea, things went better than expected. I ended up winning the entire contest for *Best Original Idea of 2011*. Sure, there was a financial award, but that wasn't the real win. The real value came from the connections I made with angel investors, venture capitalists, and mentors who showed me how to develop, pitch, and bring a concept to life. That experience was priceless.

Because at the end of the day, people who truly Reset Their Mindset don't just *see* possibilities—they *seize* them. They move from observation to ownership, from complaint to contribution, from awareness to action. That's the shift.

CHAPTER 16
INCOME OR OUTCOME

Income: The financial gain received in exchange for services rendered. In the context of leadership or instruction, income represents the monetary return, tuition, promotion fees, subscriptions, or revenue streams that sustain a business or teaching platform.

Outcome: The measurable growth, transformation, and development in the lives of those you lead. In teaching or leadership, the outcome is the impact—the confidence gained, character built, skills developed, and values instilled through intentional guidance.

The first karate tournament I ever attended wasn't just a competition—it was a revelation.

After three years of training, I finally stepped into that buzzing gymnasium, filled with the electricity of movement, discipline, and anticipation. There were competitors of every age, from tiny white belts to seasoned tenth-degree black belts. The mats were alive with action: sparring matches, board-breaking events, and kata demonstrations unfolding in every corner. It was everything I'd imagined—and more.

But as exciting as the competition was, it wasn't the trophies or techniques that stuck with me. It was a realization. A quiet, personal revelation about what kind of instructor I had, and what type of instructor I wanted to be.

My instructor didn't spend the day marketing his school or handing out flyers. He wasn't there to network or recruit. He was *all in* on me and the few students who came to compete. Every correction he offered, every word of encouragement, every piece of feedback—it was clear: my growth was his priority. Not his brand. Not his bank account. *Me.*

That day, I also got a glimpse into another world—the opposite side of that mindset. I couldn't help but notice other schools represented at the tournament. Their students looked sharp in their uniforms and carried high-level ranks on their belts. But once they stepped on the mat... something didn't add up. The skills didn't match the stripes. The belts said black, but the techniques said beginner.

It was eye-opening. Some of those students were clearly promoted far too quickly, likely for reasons that had little to do with merit and everything to do with money. They weren't being trained. They were being *processed.* It was a heartbreaking realization: in some dojos, rank had become a revenue stream rather than a reflection of readiness.

That day, the difference between *income* and *outcome* became very real to me. One instructor cared more about *transformation* than transaction. Others seemed more focused on the *promotion fee* than the person being promoted.

That tournament planted a seed in me—one that would shape how I lead, teach, and serve for years to come. I saw with my own eyes what happens when you teach for *outcome*, not just *income*. I felt what it meant to be under a leader who cared more about what I became than what I paid.

And I quietly promised myself: if I ever found myself in the position of instructor, mentor, or leader, I would be the kind who invests in *people,* not just programs. I'd ensure that any belt my students wore wasn't just wrapped around their waist, but one that had been earned through their sweat, growth, and transformation.

I opened Hickory Bushido Martial Arts in 2010, and I recall a night when the dojo was quiet. The mats were clean, the uniforms were hung, and the bills… well, the bills were still due. As a martial arts instructor, there comes a point where you stand on the mat and understand there is an intersection of two powerful forces—*income* and *outcome*. One keeps the lights on. The other keeps your purpose alive.

At first glance, these two goals might seem like opposing forces: one pulling you toward financial stability, the other calling you to higher service. But leadership—true, transformational leadership—is not about choosing one or the other. It's about anchoring your life in the outcome, knowing that income is a byproduct, not the purpose.

Let's be clear. Income isn't bad. You need it to pay rent, buy groceries, support your family, and yes, keep your school open. But the danger comes when income becomes the *goal* instead of the *result*. When leadership becomes transactional, students become customers, and your mission shrinks to maintaining subscriptions, rather than shaping souls.

It's easy to slip into this mindset:
- Pushing for belt promotions too soon to keep students engaged and paying.
- Prioritizing flash over form to "sell" the class to parents.
- Watering down values to avoid conflict, keep peace, and prevent cancellations.

In the short term, these strategies might boost the bank account. But over time, they starve the spirit—yours and theirs. The irony? The more you chase money, the more elusive it becomes. People can feel when you're serving them or when you're selling to them.

When you focus on *outcome*, on the transformation of those you lead, you tap into something much more profound.

You don't just teach martial arts, you instill discipline. You don't just teach self-defense, you inspire self-respect. You're not just collecting tuition, you're developing courage, character, and confidence.

Outcome-driven leadership asks:
- Are my students growing, or just going through the motions?
- Am I forming black belts in skill, or in life?
- Is my mission to produce excellent athletes—or excellent people?

When you teach with purpose, lead with vision, and serve with heart, you become more than an instructor—you become a mentor, a guide, a difference-maker. And ironically, *that's what people pay for.* Not the kicks or the kata, but an experience that forms character.

Here's the mindset shift: don't teach for what you can *get* from your students, teach for what you can *give* to your students. When you start by giving time, wisdom, and intentional care, the return follows: maybe not instantly, maybe not in the way you expect, but consistently, faithfully, and abundantly over time.

Transformation isn't scalable in the way profits are, but it's far more sustaining. One life changed for the better often becomes your greatest referral. One student who finds confidence because of your class tells a friend, who tells their parent, who brings their child, who becomes your next black belt. And guess what? Your income grew, but your *impact* grew faster.

Jesus once said, *"Whoever wants to become great among you must be your servant."* The path to greatness isn't paved in paychecks—it's marked by people. A servant-hearted leader doesn't ignore their needs. They just don't *prioritize* them over the mission.

That doesn't mean neglecting your responsibilities. You still need to steward your resources effectively—budget wisely, set tuition rates, and charge what your value is worth. But your *why* isn't income. Its outcome. And that mindset shift recalibrates everything.

Let's not pretend it's easy. Bills don't pause for noble intentions. Groceries don't wait on breakthroughs. But living in the tension between income and outcome is where faith grows, character is refined, and legacy is built.

So how do you do it?

- Revisit your mission regularly. Ask yourself: "Why did I start teaching in the first place?"
- Measure more than money. Track growth—in student lives, in relationships, in community.
- Serve first, promote second. Let your outcomes do the marketing.
- Trust the process. Income follows excellence. Excellence follows service.

In the end, income is about success. But the outcome is about significance. One feeds your wallet. The other feeds your soul.

Don't build a brand, build people. Don't just offer a program, offer transformation. When you choose *outcome* over *income*, you may not become the richest in your industry, but you will become one of the most respected. In a world full of noise and transactions, that is worth everything.

CHAPTER 17
CULTURE OR CHRIST

Culture: the shared beliefs, behaviors, or social environment connected with a particular aspect of society.

*Christi: the title given to **Jesus of Nazareth**, signifying His role as the Messiah (meaning "Anointed One") and Savior in Christian belief.*

In 2002, Rick Warren's book, The Purpose Driven Life, burst onto the scene at a time when self-help books and personal empowerment messages dominated the cultural landscape. As of 2022, it has sold over fifty million copies worldwide and has been translated into more than eighty-five languages, extending its reach across diverse cultures and nations. The book sparked the Purpose Driven Movement, which inspired churches, individuals, and organizations to focus on living with intentionality based on five Biblical purposes: worship, fellowship, discipleship, ministry, and mission. The book resonated with a post 9/11 world searching for meaning, providing hope and clarity in uncertain times. The Purpose Driven Life brought faith-based language into public discourse, influencing leaders, celebrities, and individuals across various walks of life.

In a world constantly shouting for our attention, <u>The Purpose Driven Life</u> dared to whisper something radical. The very first sentence of the book reads: *"It's not about you."* This countercultural proclamation was like a lightning bolt, jolting people out of their self-centered pursuits. This sentence reveals a deep conflict we face daily. Culture insists on shaping our identity, dictating our values, and defining our success. It pushes us to conform, celebrate self-sufficiency, and seek validation in the temporary. Yet, within every soul lies an inner voice, calling us to something higher and more enduring. It whispers truths about surrender, service, and living for something beyond ourselves. The tension between these two forces – culture's norms and Christ's call – is one of the greatest struggles of our time. The question is, which will you choose?

I am intentionally writing this chapter last, though it may be the most relevant and vital chapter of the entire book for many readers. Reset Your Mindset is my first attempt at publishing a book, and I hope to write a follow-up that reveals practical methodologies on how to achieve significance in our culture as Christians.

If you do not currently identify yourself as a Christian, I would like to invite you to continue reading through the rest of this chapter. What do you have to lose? At the very least, you will gain insight from someone who strives with intentionality to be a better husband, dad, and leader in our society.

If you identify as a Christian, I invite you to read on from a position of humility. Even if you are a Christian who is labeled by others as mature in your walk, I have a question I would like to ask all Christians. It's one that was asked of me years ago, that set me on a path of passion for creating a renewal movement of discipleship. "Are you trying to be a Christian without being a disciple?" Wait! Reread that question and contemplate your answer.

There comes a point in every life when the mirror cracks. When the methods we trusted, the advice we followed, and the systems we bought into don't deliver. The parties get old. The applause fades. The promotions don't fulfill. The self-help books become another unread stack. The same loop plays again: strive, stumble, reset, repeat.

But what if it wasn't just about another reset? What if it was about choosing a different foundation entirely?

Culture is a master persuader. It shapes how we dress, think, post, react, and dream. It demands that we constantly evolve—new opinions, new labels, new truths. Yet for all its power, culture is historically fragile. Empires have risen, ruled, and crumbled—Rome, Egypt, Babylon, and Greece. Their ideas were once gospel, too… until they weren't. Culture shifts, but Christ stands.

Consider this: for over 2,000 years, the message of Jesus Christ has endured. Not as a passing trend, but as a truth so deep, it has outlasted kingdoms, weathered criticism, and converted skeptics—many of them brilliant minds, hardened hearts, or lost souls. Even science and archaeology, disciplines once used to discredit the Bible, continue to unearth evidence that confirms its accuracy. Historical figures once thought to be mythical have been proven to be real. Ancient customs and cities once mocked in Scripture have been found. As time passes, the truth of Christianity is increasingly echoed even outside faith circles.

If you're looking for something that lasts, that works, shouldn't you consider the One who made you? When your phone breaks, you don't ask your friend who once watched a repair video. You go to the manufacturer. When you want to understand a home's structure, you talk to the builder. So, when your life feels off course, why not consult your Creator?

You were made with intention, not by accident. *"Before I formed you in the womb I knew you, before you were born, I set you apart; I appointed you as a prophet to the nations."* (Jeremiah 1:5). You were born with purpose, not randomness. And your soul, no matter how far it's drifted, was designed to find its home in Christ.

The Ten Commandments aren't outdated rules— they're reasonable boundaries. Don't steal. Don't lie. Don't cheat. Don't kill. Respect your parents. Protect your marriage. Take a day to rest. Love God. Honor truth. These aren't culture chains. They're God's loving guardrails.

And Christ? He didn't come to chain you—He came to free you. He didn't come to condemn you—He came to forgive you. Maybe you've tried everything else. Perhaps culture's promises have left you feeling empty, broken, and disillusioned. You've done it your way, and it didn't work. Could it be time to try His way? Jesus said, *"Come to me, all who are weary and burdened, and I will give you rest."* (Matthew 11:28)

If you feel tired of searching, striving, and performing, He's inviting you into something different. Something real. Eternal. Not religion. Not rituals. A Relationship. And here's the beautiful part: God's been pursuing you all along. Even in the moments you ignored Him, resisted Him, or ran from Him, He never stopped loving you. He's been drawing you closer through every high and low, waiting patiently for you to realize He's what you've been searching for all along.

So, as you reach the final pages of this book, I want to gently ask:

Would you be willing to admit that you're a sinner—that your way hasn't worked?
Would you be willing to ask for forgiveness?
Would you accept the love and mercy of Jesus Christ, who died so you could live?
Would you be open to making Him not just your Savior, but your Lord?

It's not about positive mental attitude, memorizing a list of rules, or pretending to be perfect. It's about surrender.

About trust. About letting the One who made you transform you into your full potential and purpose. If your heart says yes, you don't need fancy words. Just a sincere prayer:

"Jesus, I admit I've sinned. I've tried it my way, and I'm still empty. I believe You died for me, and I believe You rose again. Please forgive me. Come into my life. Be my Lord and my Savior. I give my life to You."

That's it.

Resetting your mindset might start with a thought, but real transformation begins with a decision. *Culture* may offer moments, but *Christ* offers eternity. Which will you choose?